Effective Use of Collective Peer Teaching in Teacher Education

Effective Use of Collective Peer Teaching in Teacher Education investigates the learning benefits of letting students assume leadership roles in the classroom, emphasizing both theoretical analysis and first-hand empirical research conducted with pre-service teachers.

Building on Vygotsky's (1987) sociocultural theory of human learning and research on collective intelligence, this volume introduces peer teaching as a pedagogical practice with a significant and underexplored learning potential. The first part of this book focuses on findings from two separate teacher education programs, while the second analyzes the learning processes through three conceptualized learning positions: peer teacher learning, peer student learning, and collective peer learning. Investigating the balance and interaction of these processes, this book argues that teaching and learning cannot at length be separated from each other and discusses the practical implications of this idea.

This book will appeal to researchers, faculty, and teacher educators with interests in theories of learning and international and comparative education. Its crucial insights into how learning can be maximized in the classroom will provide a nuanced picture of the complexity of learning processes.

Rolf K. Baltzersen is a Professor in the Faculty of Education and International Studies at Oslo Metropolitan University, Norway.

Routledge Research in Teacher Education

The Routledge Research in Teacher Education series presents the latest research on Teacher Education and also provides a forum to discuss the latest practices and challenges in the field.

Moral and Political Values in Teacher Education Over Time
International Perspectives
Edited by Nick Mead

Middle Level Teacher Preparation across International Contexts
Understanding Local and Global Factors Influencing Teacher Education
Edited by Cheryl R. Ellerbrock, Katherine M. Main, and David C. Virtue

Reconceptualizing Early Career Teacher Mentoring as Reggio-Inspired
Insights from Collaborative Research with Art Teachers
Christina Hanawalt and Brooke Hofsess

Accommodating Marginalized Students in Higher Education
A Structural Theory Approach
W.P. Wahl and Louis H. Falik

Innovation in Teacher Professional Learning in Europe
Research, Policy and Practice
Edited by Ken Jones, Giorgio Ostinelli, and Alberto Crescentini

Effective Use of Collective Peer Teaching in Teacher Education
Maximizing Student Learning
Rolf K. Baltzersen

For more information about this series, please visit: https://www.routledge.com/Routledge-Research-in-Teacher-Education/book-series/RRTE

Effective Use of Collective Peer Teaching in Teacher Education
Maximizing Student Learning

Rolf K. Baltzersen

First published 2024
by Routledge
605 Third Avenue, New York, NY 10158

and by Routledge
4 Park Square, Milton Park, Abingdon, Oxon, OX14 4RN

Routledge is an imprint of the Taylor & Francis Group, an informa business

© 2024 Rolf K. Baltzersen

The right of Rolf K. Baltzersen to be identified as author of this work has been asserted in accordance with sections 77 and 78 of the Copyright, Designs and Patents Act 1988.

"The Open Access version of this book, available at www.taylorfrancis. com, has been made available under a Creative Commons [Attribution-Non-Commercial-No Derivatives (CC-BY-NC-ND)] 4.0 license.

Funded by Oslo Metropolitan University."

Trademark notice: Product or corporate names may be trademarks or registered trademarks, and are used only for identification and explanation without intent to infringe.

ISBN: 978-1-032-51346-1 (hbk)
ISBN: 978-1-032-51726-1 (pbk)
ISBN: 978-1-003-40358-6 (ebk)

DOI: 10.4324/9781003403586

Typeset in Times New Roman
by codeMantra

Contents

1 **What is collective peer teaching**   1
   The origins of learning by teaching   1
   Modern research on peer teaching   2
   A typology of peer teaching   5
      Formal peer teaching in smaller groups within the whole group   5
      Informal peer teaching in smaller groups within the whole group   7
      Informal peer teaching of the whole group   7
      Formal peer teaching of the whole group   8
      From microteaching to collective peer teaching   9
   The three learning positions in peer teaching   10
      Peer student learning   10
      Peer teacher learning   10
      Collective peer learning   11
      Why this book matters: the central purpose   12

2 **Qualitative review—formal peer teaching of the whole group**   13
   A qualitative systematic review   13
      Review aim   13
      Search methodology   14
      An overview of selected studies   15
      Review analysis   16
   Article nr.1—Velez et al. (2011)   17
      About the instructional design and the research study   17
      Peer teacher learning   18
      Peer student learning   18
      Collective peer learning   19

Article nr.2—Moust and Schmidt (1994) 20
　　The instructional design and the research study 20
　　Peer student learning 21
Article nr.3—Lockspeiser et al. (2008) 24
　　The instructional design and the research study 24
　　Peer student learning 25
　　Peer teacher learning 27
　　Collective peer learning 27
Article nr.4—Aslan (2015) 28
　　The instructional design and the research study 28
　　Peer teacher learning 29
　　Collective peer learning 30
　　Peer student learning 30
Article nr.5—Aslan (2017a) 31
　　The instructional design and the research study 31
　　Peer teacher learning 31
Article nr.6—Aslan (2017b) 32
　　The instructional design and the research study 32
　　Peer teacher learning 33
Summary of the review 33
　　Review of peer teacher learning 34
　　Review of peer student learning 35
　　Review of collective peer learning 36
　　How will this review be used? 37

3　First case study—collective peer teaching in teacher education　39
　The collective peer teaching design 39
　The research study 40
　Peer student learning 41
　　Academic learning (the subject matter) 42
　Peer teacher learning 45
　　Strong student motivation 46
　　Deep learning 46
　　Learning through co-teaching 47
　　Improving teaching skills 48
　　Interest in peer teaching as a teaching method 48
　Collective peer learning 49
　　Increasing lesson diversity 49
　　A community of equals 50
　　Learning by switching roles 51

  Scaling up the peer feedback 52
  Developing knowledge collectively 53

4 Second case study—collective peer teaching in teacher education   55
 The collective peer teaching design 55
 The research study 56
 Peer student learning 57
  Professionally relevant learning 57
  Academic learning 58
  Active learning 59
  Relevance for the summative assessment 59
 Peer teacher learning 59
 Collective peer learning 62
  Professional learning community 62
  The organization of the lessons 62
  The benefits of observational learning 62
  Collective peer feedback 63
  Class atmosphere 63
  Fair learning 64

5 Perspectives on peer teacher learning   65
 Higher-order thinking skills 65
  Background 65
  Learning by asking reflective questions (during the lesson) 66
  Learning by explaining 66
  Learning by summarizing 67
  Learning metacognitive skills 68
 Acquisition of professional skills 70
  Improving your teaching skills 70
  Peer teacher collaboration 71
 Peer teacher motivation 71
  Social responsibility and performance anxiety 71
  Mastery of the lesson 72
  Peer teacher interests 73
  Motivation and formal assessment 75
 Iterative learning 75
  Preparation phase 75
  Enactment phase 76

viii Contents

> Post-lesson phase 77
> Moving through different modes of reflection 79
> Summary—peer teacher learning as deep learning 80

6 **Perspectives on peer student learning** 83
> Introduction 83
> Relevant lesson content 84
> Relevance for the summative assessment 86
> Whole-class discussions (dialogic teaching) 87
> Engaging teaching (other teaching methods) 88
> Proximity as the fundamental characteristic of peer student learning? 88
>> The zone of cognitive proximity 90
>> The zone of social proximity 91

7 **Perspectives on collective peer learning** 93
> Introduction 93
> Whole-group structure 93
>> Switching positions 93
>> Fair division of work 95
> Whole-group relations 95
> Whole-group knowledge 96
>> Sharing of whole-group knowledge in a face-to-face setting 96
>> Sharing of whole-group knowledge in an online setting 98
> Whole-group feedback 99
>> The learning value of receiving peer feedback 99
>> Evaluation of the collective peer teaching design 101
> Whole-group diversity 101
>> Increasing the number of lessons 101
>> Increasing the diversity of teaching styles 102
>> Increasing the lesson content diversity 104
>> Increasing the diversity of the quality of teaching 104
> Summary—collective peer learning as collective intelligence 106
>> Rotation 106
>> Community of student experts 107
>> Collective knowledge advancement 108
>> Collective peer evaluation 110

The wisdom of the student crowd 111
  Collective peer teaching as human swarm
    problem-solving 113

8 **Conclusion—final remarks** 115
  The interplay between the three learning positions 115
  Transforming campus into practice—implications
    for teacher education 118

  Appendix *119*
  Refference *127*
  Index *133*

1 What is collective peer teaching

The origins of learning by teaching

The principal question this book seeks to explore is: does teaching indeed constitute the most potent form of learning? This question will underpin the discourse of all the chapters herein. Reference to the Learning Pyramid often highlights the act of teaching as an exceptional method of learning. However, this Pyramid has been met with criticism due to its lack of empirical evidence (Letrud & Hernes, 2018; Masters, 2013).

Reflecting on the historical roots of learning by teaching, the figure of John Amos Comenius (1592–1670) emerges as a notably intriguing educational philosopher. Recognized as the "father of modern education," Comenius pioneered the use of textbooks and was the advocate for universal education. However, a less widely known aspect of his philosophy is his critique of the pedagogical practices of his era for their failure to let students assume the role of teachers. He firmly believed teaching in schools should not keep things apart that naturally belong together. For instance, in primary schools, children were taught to read, with writing instruction deferred for several months. In the Latin School, boys spent years learning grammar, words without any reference to their meanings. Comenius contended that reading and writing, words and their meanings, and learning and teaching are intrinsically interconnected and cannot exist in isolation (Comenius, 1896, p. 313).

To illustrate his point, Comenius offered this comparison: "(…), just as, in running, the raising of the feet is combined with the setting of them on the ground again, or, in conversation, listening is combined with answering, or, in playing ball, throwing is combined with catching" (Comenius, 1896, p. 313). He advocated for the immediate application of new knowledge, noting, "Whatever has been learned should be communicated by one pupil to the other, that no knowledge may remain unused" (Comenius, 1896, p. 307). In this sense, teaching becomes a necessity for learning, as students who acquire new knowledge should be able to explain or impart it to others.

Comenius referenced a well-known Latin couplet to bolster his argument: "To ask many questions, to retain the answers, and to teach what one retains to

DOI: 10.4324/9781003403586-1

This chapter has been made available under a CC-BY-NC-ND 4.0 license.

2 What is collective peer teaching

others; These three enable the pupil to surpass his master" (Comenius, 1896, p. 308). He distinguishes between the stages of questioning, where a student seeks clarification from teachers, peers, or texts on unfamiliar subjects, and retention, with information being remembered or written down for greater security. The final stage is teaching, where the newly acquired knowledge is shared with peers or others. Comenius believed that while schools were proficient in the first two stages, they lacked appreciation for the crucial third stage – learning by teaching, which he considered highly desirable (Comenius, 1896, pp. 308–309).

The phrase "surpass his master" suggests the transformative potential of this learning method. Comenius advanced the compelling argument that teaching is not merely an act of imparting knowledge but also a learning experience in itself, "He who teaches others, teaches himself" (Comenius, 1896, p. 309). This is not only because constant repetition of facts has a stronger influence on the mind, but because the process of teaching in itself gives a deeper insight into the subject taught. Here, he refers to the humanist Joachim Fortius who used to say that "if he had heard or read anything once, it slipped out of his memory within a month; but that if he taught it to others it became as much a part of himself as his fingers (…)" (Comenius, 1896, p. 309). Fortius recommended that students who wanted to make progress should give lessons daily in the subjects they were studying, even if they had to hire students to participate. To get someone to listen while you were teaching was the same as making intellectual progress (Comenius, 1896, p. 309).

To Comenius, the teacher should motivate and encourage students to seek out and obtain intellectual food by themselves, assimilate and digest it, and then share it with others (Comenius, 1896, p. 308). For large classes, he proposed the most effective strategy would be to arrange students into smaller groups that can mutually support, instruct, and monitor each other, thus promoting a chain of learning and teaching (Zuckerman, 2021). This arrangement, he posited, would foster an environment conducive to reciprocal learning and teaching.

Modern research on peer teaching

In essence, Comenius' educational philosophy revolved around the notion that education should not merely involve passive absorption of information but should instead support active learners who can synthesize their knowledge and share it with others. The act of teaching, in his view, was essential in deep learning. His perspectives, revolutionary in their time, continue to be relevant. However, Zuckerman (2021) asks why this part of Comenius pedagogical thinking has been neglected and lacked influence in schools? On the one hand, she claims this is not entirely true. In small, rural schools, where teachers might struggle to address the needs of students of different ages simultaneously, employing students as peer teachers could be more effective It is the same in a family with many children, when adults are unable to cope with their household, they let older children mentor the younger ones. Here, peer teaching arises out of necessity, but in ordinary schools, it appears to be only the most talented teachers who prefer this pedagogical approach (Zuckerman, 2021).

On the other hand, learning by teaching have in recent years received more attention among educational researchers (Duran, 2017; Duran & Topping, 2017; Topping et al., 2017). One reason is the groundbreaking work by John Hattie (2009). He synthesized over 800 meta-analyses and concluded that "the remarkable feature of the evidence is that the biggest effects on student learning occur when teachers become learners of their own teaching, and when students become their own teachers" (Hattie, 2009, p. 22). He finds that when students can monitor their own journey of learning from idea development to a complete understanding, they become teachers of their own learning. It is all about making both learning and teaching more visible. Here, the notion of a student as their own teacher primarily involves the development of metacognitive skills such as self-monitoring, self-evaluation, self-assessment, and self-teaching. Although Hattie's focus lies predominantly on self-teaching as opposed to "teaching others," his research indicates that these two learning activities are related to each other.

According to Puchner (2003), peer teaching is any activity where students take on a teaching role in the school setting, doing activities that professional teachers normally do. This includes presenting, mentoring, facilitating, demonstrating, telling, asking questions, and explaining material to others.

With such a broad understanding, the peer teaching period can vary a lot in scope and duration from a brief answer to a question, to a whole lesson or even a complete course (Duran, 2017; Falchikov, 2001; Hanke, 2012; Topping & Ehly, 1998; Topping et al., 2017). Several typologies aim to provide a broad overview (Duran, 2017; Topping et al., 2017). For instance, Duran (2017) suggests that the following pedagogical practices should be included in "learning by teaching" as a research area: (a) developing educational materials, (b) cooperative learning, (c) peer tutoring, students learning by teaching peers, (d) peer feedback (peer assessment), (e) students acting as co-teachers, and (f) learning by replacing the teacher in front of the class.

Within learning by teaching as a research area, several different terms are used which often are quite similar in their meaning. For example, both the term peer teaching and the term peer tutoring are educational strategies that refer to students learning from and with each other. The term peer teaching will often involve a more formal, instructional relationship, with one student taking on the role of the teacher, while peer tutoring focuses on a more collaborative relationship, with the tutor providing guidance as needed.

4 *What is collective peer teaching*

In peer teaching, the student takes on the role of the "teacher," being responsible for instructing their fellow students or peers. This peer teacher is expected to have a higher level of understanding in the subject being taught. It resembles what Duran (2017) labels as "Learning by replacing the teacher in front of the class." The learning process is typically more structured and formalized, with the peer teacher using a lesson plan and making the instructional material. The goal is to help the peer students develop an understanding of the subject matter.

In peer tutoring, the focus is more on collaborative learning in a more symmetrical learning relationship. Topping (1996) defines peer tutoring as "people from similar social groupings who are not professional teachers helping each other to learn and learn themselves by teaching." The peer tutor may still have more expertise but will to a greater degree support and guide the tutee on problems the student is struggling with. Less time is used for formalized instruction, but the emphasis is more on individualized support, tailored to the tutee's needs. The group size varies, including both pairs and larger student groups. Furthermore, it is possible to distinguish between cross-age or cross-level tutoring and same-age or same-level tutoring, with peer tutors either being at a higher or the same educational level. In addition, peer tutoring may be fixed with one member always performing the role of tutor, or reciprocal, with students switching on the peer tutor roles, either being tutor or being tutee (Topping, 2005).

Peer tutoring is typically a supplement to the formal teaching, while peer teaching will more often be a replacement of this teaching. To a greater degree, peer teaching is directed toward a larger student group within school hours, usually a school class. Classroom management will also be necessary. In comparison, a tutor will follow up students one-to-one or in smaller groups. Teaching methods are adjusted to individual students with more immediate feedback and flexible learning schedules (Duran, 2017; Falchikov, 2001; Hanke, 2012; Topping et al., 2017).

Peer tutoring often supplements the formal teaching by filling in gaps in knowledge or supporting the development of more specific skills. In educational systems, peer tutoring is widely used in medical schools to support students in the laboratory. The tutors are usually junior doctors or upper classmen. Although tutors are not required to have formal teaching qualifications, they usually have qualifications in the subjects by previously having passed the exam (Evans & Cuffe, 2009; Rees et al., 2016). In some programs, both peer tutoring and peer teaching may be available. For example, in medical school, students can be offered both one-on-one peer tutoring and peer teaching in a large group setting. The goal is to reduce drop-out rates and improve academic performance (Lockspeiser et al., 2008).

Note also that the conceptual relationship between peer tutoring and peer teaching is not clear-cut and the terms overlap. For example, in some cases, peer tutoring will often be very similar to peer teaching with strong elements of instruction combined with individual guidance and support.

A typology of peer teaching

In this book, a new typology is introduced which describes peer teaching as a broader concept than what is usual, including both peer tutoring and collaborative learning in smaller groups. The first dimension distinguishes between formal and informal teaching. On the one hand, *formal peer teaching* is organized around predefined roles and rules for social interaction between the students. It usually requires lesson planning and that the teacher explain what the students are expected to do. On the other hand, *informal peer teaching* is more spontaneous and does not follow the same predefined interactional rules. This teaching will often emerge as a need in the situation in the ongoing work, by giving explanations or having informal discussions. Depending on how the interaction unfolds, any student can provide informal teaching by answering questions or explaining issues. This informal peer teaching resembles what Topping et al. (2017) label as mutual peer learning, being student-centered with little degree of formal teacher intervention.

The second dimension distinguishes between the *whole group (or class) vs smaller group within the whole group.* Here, the notion of the "whole group" includes peer teaching of a large group of 20–30 students and a smaller group of 5–10 students. This term is perhaps not so different from what Duran (2017) labels as "learning by replacing the teacher in front of the class," a distinct subtype within learning by teaching. Table 1.1 summarizes this two-dimensional typology of peer teaching with different examples.

Formal peer teaching in smaller groups within the whole group

There are a multitude of different ways to organize formal peer teaching in smaller groups within a class. One of the most well-known teaching methods is cooperative learning which first gives students time to learn about a topic before they teach this content to others in a small group (Johnson, 1994; Johnson & Johnson, 2018). In this structured setting, all group members are assigned to act as teachers for each other in small groups. Equal participation by all group members is important. In addition, it is encouraged to use strategies such as summarizing, questioning, explaining, argumentation, and disagreement (Topping et al., 2017). The jigsaw is another example of a teaching method that allows for students to be teachers for each other in small groups by first acquiring knowledge about one part of the material (Ab Murat, 2018). In "reciprocal teaching" (Palinscar & Brown, 1984), students are assigned to summarize the main ideas and teach them to their peers. When learners know that they are going to teach a peer, they often read with a stronger intention of understanding the content (Topping et al., 2017). In reciprocal peer tutoring, pairs of students with similar educational background assist each other in the academic learning process (Gazula et al., 2017).

Table 1.1 A typology of peer teaching: A comparison of formal vs informal peer teaching and class group size

	Smaller group within the whole group (or class)	The whole group (or class)
Formal peer teaching (roles and rules of interaction are predefined)	- Alternative 1: Rule-governed collaborative interaction where students learn the material and then teach the rest of the group: cooperative learning, reciprocal teaching, jigsaw method, and reciprocal peer tutoring. - Alternative 2: Peer assessment that let students assess each other's work.	- Alternative 1: "Same-level" collective peer teaching. All students in the same group are involved in being peer teachers for each other. Students usually rotate on being in the role of peer teacher. - Alternative 2: "Cross-level" peer teaching of a whole student group or class. This near-peer teaching is led by students at a higher educational level and is often labeled as peer tutoring. Peer tutors have normally completed the course they are teaching, and the same person is usually a peer teacher throughout the course.
Informal peer teaching (teaching is part of the discourse and not a separate role)	- A number of activities during collaboration in group work can be labeled as informal peer teaching. This involves activities such as informing others, explaining, and answering questions. It usually emerges spontaneously as part of the problem-solving process and knowledge sharing during the group work.	- Sharing of knowledge between all students in the group at a plenary level, not only in smaller groups in the class. This learning activity is present in several different pedagogical approaches, such as project-based learning, problem-based learning, and challenge-based learning.

Another well-known example is the peer instruction method developed by Eric Mazur, which emphasizes proximity to the process of solving the problem. The instructional design centers around the assumption that the best teacher is the person who has just recently solved a problem. Through small group discussions of specific assignments and puzzles, students try and convince each other by explaining the reasons behind their proposed solution. They are encouraged to find somebody who proposes an alternative answer. Although the teacher explanation will usually be the most efficient route from question to answer, the student explanations are often more convincing. Peer explanations will also be different because students are usually not certain about whether the explanation is correct. In contrast, it is expected that the teacher will always communicate the correct answer (Crouch et al., 2007).

In addition, formal peer teaching in small groups can be conducted as peer assessment which let student groups assess each other's work (Duran, 2017; Topping, 2009). Here, specific typical teaching behaviors are transferred to the students. Peer assessment is an arrangement that let learners consider and specify the level, value, or quality of a product or performance of other equal-status learners. A wide variety of products can be assessed, including writing, portfolios, oral presentations, test performance, and other skilled behaviors. The goal of peer assessment is often to improve student performance through both written and oral feedback. The benefit of using peers is that they will usually have more time to provide detailed support (Topping, 2009). Students learn both by giving feedback on other's work and by receiving feedback on their work (Duran & Topping, 2017; Topping et al., 2017).

Informal peer teaching in smaller groups within the whole group

Here, informal peer teaching refers to teaching-like behaviors that are not part of the formal instructional design, but emerge through the interaction itself with students helping each other while they are solving a task (Henze, 1992; Whitman & Fife, 1988). In small groups, informal peer teaching will be an integral part of the collaboration and involve many different types of helping activities that support the ongoing work. It can be to explain an issue, answer a question, make suggestions, or verbalize your own thoughts by "thinking aloud." Often, all parties in the collaboration will switch on being informal teachers. Pairs of students who collaborate will naturally alternate on asking and answering questions. During their work, they will easily observe each other's work and comment on it continuously. Because of the mutual participation, this informal teaching is often dialogical and cannot be separated from the ongoing verbal discourse (Baltzersen, 2017, pp. 237–253).

Informal peer teaching of the whole group

If we look at informal peer teaching in the whole group, the activities may be quite similar to what happens in small groups. It will typically occur in a student project which involves the whole class. Then students may help each other by informing others or answering different types of question. In larger groups, it becomes even more important to use tools that support the sharing of information to everyone such as a projector or a blackboard (Baltzersen, 2017, pp. 323–325). Because the group is larger, this type of peer teaching will to a larger degree demand the attention of all students in the group, but it will still be an integral part of the ongoing work. One example can be attempts to summarize what collective work the group has done until now (Baltzersen, 2017, pp. 226–231). In the knowledge-building pedagogy, the collective work of the entire class is shared in various ways. This includes attempts to

8 *What is collective peer teaching*

evaluate, critically examine, and further develop ideas through whole-class discussions (Scardamalia & Bereiter, 2006). Although not labeled as informal peer teaching, it will be integrated in most type of collective student work, whether it is project-based learning (Kokotsaki et al., 2016), problem-based learning (Moust et al., 2021; Yew & Goh, 2016) or challenge-based learning (Gallagher & Savage, 2020).

Formal peer teaching of the whole group

Formal peer teaching of the whole group (or class) resembles what Duran (2017) describes as "students replacing the teacher in front of the class." It differs from a simple oral presentation because the peer teacher involves the students in different kinds of learning activities. It will usually be enough time to present a new subject and lead whole-class discussions. Here, there are two distinctly different subtypes, cross-level peer teaching with peer teachers being at a higher educational level, and same-level collective peer teaching, where all students switch on being peer teachers for each other.

On the one hand, *cross-level peer teaching* is very common in many educational settings in higher education. A peer teacher is usually permanently responsible for helping a group of students throughout a course. This is typically a more experienced student, often a graduate student being responsible for undergraduate courses (Topping et al., 2017). Because the peer teacher has passed the relevant exam, this person will have more advanced skills and knowledge about the subject matter. In addition, the peer teachers are often handpicked among the best students to ensure optimal teaching quality. Although these peer teachers are often paid, the salary is much lower compared with faculty teachers. This is why the use of peer teachers have been regarded as beneficial from an economic perspective.

On the other hand, *same-level collective peer teaching* let all student rotate on being peer teachers during a course, independent of their background knowledge level or skill level. At its most basic level, the instructional design facilitates learning processes between students without a formal teacher being at the center of attention. The arguably most prominent example of collective peer teaching is the 'Lernen durch Lehren' approach developed by Jean Pol Martin in foreign language teaching in Germany in the 1980s. Martin experimented with giving students shared responsibility for French lessons and observed that their new role motivated them to engage in more intensive and authentic communication. By letting all students take turns on teaching the whole class, students learned the language through a different type of verbal interaction (Martin, 2018). What is special with collective peer teaching, is that it challenges our fundamental assumption about how teaching should be done, including the social positions in the classroom and its power structures. It is likely that this is the main reason that it appears to be such a rare practice in formal education. Note that the notion of collective peer teaching is also a new term introduced in this book, to capture the characteristics of this unique pedagogical practice.

From microteaching to collective peer teaching

The typology of peer teaching does not only provide an overview of the complexity of peer teaching, but the inclusion of both formal and informal peer teaching shows that it covers a wide range of pedagogical practices. In the review in the next chapter, the selected studies only involve one of the subtypes, *formal peer teaching of the whole group (or class)*. Although there is a concern about the quality of the peer teaching, Topping et al. (2017, p. 22) still summarize the empirical research by recommending that all students should be allowed to be peer tutors (peer teachers). While cooperative learning involves all students in teaching-like behaviors, most of these activities happen in small groups. It is less common with collective peer teaching that let students switch on being responsible for the whole class and replace the teacher for a substantial amount of the teaching time. Until now, few studies have analyzed what happens when all students are assigned to be teachers for each other.

In the teacher education context, microteaching can be regarded as a teaching method which is affiliated with collective peer teaching. Microteaching was developed in the 1960s by Dwight Allen and his colleagues at Stanford University (Allen et al., 1972). It allowed pre-service teachers to improve their teaching skills and behaviors (e.g. using voice, tone, and mimics) by being teachers for each other at campus in a safe environment (Cavanaugh, 2022; Ralph, 2014). The class environment is simpler with a small group of peers, shorter duration of teaching, and less demands regarding the lesson content. Student teachers typically plan and present a 5- to 10-minute lesson, in which they try to apply specific instructional skills or tasks previously studied in class. It usually involves video-recording of the lesson, which allows for observation and evaluation afterward, involving both peer feedback and teacher feedback (Ralph, 2014; Sen, 2009).

Other studies have also found improvement in critical thinking (Arsal, 2015) and the ability to give peer feedback (Bakır, 2014). Ralph (2014) provides an overview of several strengths. A major advantage is practice of discrete skills in low-risk settings. It also promotes self-reflection and builds confidence. The video recording of your own teaching can be a powerful learning experience, involving both self-critical reflections, peer feedback and teacher feedback. Peers also learn by evaluating each other. The major limitation is that the emphasis is often on low-level skills, not on development of a more holistic teaching proficiency. Nor are the skills necessarily transferable to other educational contexts. Teaching in front of peers may also be more

10 *What is collective peer teaching*

stressful with peers being insensitive to each other. In contrast to collective peer teaching, it will usually not be orientated toward the lesson content.

The three learning positions in peer teaching

Broadly, research on peer teaching distinguishes between peer student learning and peer teacher learning as two separate yet crucial learning positions. However, this book posits the need for a third learning position, termed "collective peer learning," asserting its significance in peer teaching.

Peer student learning

If we first look at peer student learning, there are a number of studies that provide evidence that peer tutoring has a positive effect on the academic achievements of students at different educational levels (Bowman-Perrott et al., 2013; Leung, 2015). These effects are even larger for at-risk students (Topping etşal., 2017, p. 23). Since extracurricular peer tutoring is usually a supplement to faculty teaching, improved academic achievement is perhaps no surprise. For instance, there are much fewer studies of what happens if the peer teaching replaces parts of faculty teaching. The major concern is a potentially negative effect on academic achievement gains (Stigmar, 2016; Topping et al., 2017,p. 22). Surprisingly, a recent review by Rees et al. (2016) in medical education found no significant differences in learning outcomes when peer teaching was directly compared with faculty teaching. One explanation may be that students receive more individualized help in peer teaching compared with faculty teaching (Duran & Topping, 2017). In addition, studies of peer teaching often find that the group communication and relations are improved (Topping et al., 2017, p. 22). Still, there are few studies of peer teaching that examine in detail what is positive in peer student learning. Stigmar (2016) also recommends that the specific educational setting should be included in the analysis of learning outcomes.

Peer teacher learning

Regarding peer teacher learning, a recent meta-analysis of peer tutoring shows evidence of positive effects on tutors' academic achievement (Leung, 2019). One study even shows that high-needs children can benefit emotionally and academically, both by being tutees and by being tutors (Leung, 2015; Topping et al., 2017, p. 23). This involves not only improved understanding of the learning content, but more frequent higher-order thinking and deep-level learning (Fiorella & Mayer, 2013, 2016; Kobayashi, 2019; Roscoe, 2014; Roscoe & Chi, 2008; Topping et al., 2017, pp. 22–23). For example, in one study participants that read about a topic with the expectation of teaching it outperformed the participants that just took a comprehension test on the material. However, it was only the group that actually taught the content of a lesson, that developed a deeper and more persistent understanding of the material compared with the group that only prepared to teach (Fiorella & Mayer, 2013). Moreover, peer teacher learning is important because it can produce a wide range of other social, affective, and motivational benefits that go beyond students' academic learning. This learning involves the building of self-confidence and social competence, and the development of a more positive attitude toward school and the subject matter (Topping et al., 2017, p. 22).

Still, many of these studies are limited because they are from experimental settings. Most of the studies of peer teachers or cross-level peer tutors only involve a small group of high performers who are often more competent and motivated than other students (Topping et al., 2017, p. 23). Therefore, it is important with more studies that examine peer teaching learning in instructional design that involve all students or a more representative group (Evans & Cuffe, 2009; Rees et al., 2016). In addition, we know little about how the peer teacher learning emerges through the lesson preparation phase and during the lesson.

Collective peer learning

In this context, the term collective peer learning addresses peer-to-peer learning in a large group. In recent decades, we have witnessed a "sociocultural turn" regarding our understanding of the concept of learning. This shift has to a large degree been inspired by the work of Lev Vygotsky (1978). He claims that higher mental functioning such as language, writing, counting, drawing, and memory are all mediated by tools and signs. Language is the primary psychological tool we use to understand the world. Many scholars within the learning sciences build on this theoretical framework and highlight that learning must be understood as an interactive process based on participation in cultural practices. Learning is defined as a process of becoming a member of a community and acquiring the skills to communicate and act according to its socially negotiated norms (Lave & Wenger, 1991; Sfard, 1998). For example, in the study of creativity, it has been suggested that we should move from the idea of individual genius to the study of the social and cultural conditions that inhibit or enable creativity (Sawyer, 2006). New theories of learning also highlight the qualities of group discourse and joint meaning-making to a greater degree (Stahl, 2006). Knowledge does not reside inside the heads of individuals but in the practice itself. In addition, a set of new approaches have been employed to investigate peer-to-peer learning at a collective level, like knowledge building (Scardamalia & Bereiter, 2006) and expansive learning (Engeström, 2014).

However, these theories scarcely elaborate on the connection between teaching and learning. For example, if we look at situated learning (Lave & Wenger, 1991), near-peers are a part of the community of practice, but it is the peer learning process, not the informal peer teaching, which is highlighted. Likewise, a theory like knowledge building (Scardamalia & Bereiter, 2006) centers on peer-to-peer learning in projects which involve the whole student group. The basic pedagogical idea is to turn over increasingly higher levels of agency to the students, which are normally undertaken by the teacher. Students are challenged to evaluate the progress of their problem-solving discourse, critically examine goals, ensure inclusiveness, and find ways around obstacles (Scardamalia & Bereiter, 2006; 2014). Still, these processes are not labeled as informal peer teaching, although student explanations are essential.

Because collective peer learning is directed toward large groups like the whole student group or class, it is also relevant to include perspectives on collective intelligence. The term describes shared knowledge, skills, and problem-solving abilities that emerge when a group of individuals work together, pooling their diverse expertise to achieve a common goal. This concept highlights that the collective understanding of a group can often be more effective than the capabilities of individual members (Baltzersen, 2022). In Chapter 7, the intention is also to provide more detailed theoretical insight into the mechanisms in collective peer learning.

Why this book matters: the central purpose

In learning by teaching as a research area, sociocultural learning theories have also gained more interest in recent years. One example is a book by Duran and Topping (2017), which is inspired by Vygotskian perspectives. Still, there are few discussions of collective learning processes that involve the whole student group in the book. The most likely explanation is the general lack of studies on collective peer teaching that let all students become peer teachers.

In addressing this lack of research knowledge, collective peer teaching will in this book be analyzed as a unique type of peer teaching. All chapters in the book will center on analyzing and discussing the three previously mentioned learning positions. In the next chapter, this will be done by doing a qualitative review of formal peer teaching of the whole class. In Chapters 3 and 4, two case studies will be analyzed in relation to the three learning positions. Chapters 5, 6, and 7 will analyze this learning in a theoretical perspective. Hopefully, these discussions do not only contribute to theory development within peer teaching as a research area, but they might also help improve our more general understanding of classroom learning.

2 Qualitative review—formal peer teaching of the whole group

A qualitative systematic review

Review aim

The aim of this qualitative systematic review (Thomas & Harden, 2008) is to synthesize and interpret findings from a selection of studies that center on *formal peer teaching of the whole group*.[1] It includes studies of both cross-level peer teaching and same-level collective peer teaching.[2] The primary objective is to examine how three distinct learning positions, briefly introduced in Chapter 1, influence this teaching style. These positions are peer teacher learning, peer student learning, and collective peer learning. The selected studies' empirical findings will be reinterpreted in the context of these learning dimensions, with the goal of furthering our understanding of the complexities inherent in collective peer teaching processes.

The review's article sampling is purposive, not exhaustive, seeking to provide interpretive insights into studies that address "formal peer teaching of a whole group" (Thomas & Harden, 2008). The selection process leverages criterion sampling (Ames et al., 2019), stipulating the minimum requirement that the instructional design enables a peer teacher (or a group of peer teachers) to replace the traditional teacher in front of the class for a lesson or an extended period.

Adhering to the principle of "maximum variation sampling" (Ames et al., 2019), the review incorporates studies on cross-level peer teaching (often referred to as peer tutoring) and same-level collective peer teaching. The intent is to include a diverse range of studies to maximize the variability of peer teaching experiences (Thomas & Harden, 2008).

To enhance our comprehension of collective peer learning as a learning dimension, it was vital to incorporate the less common studies on same-level collective peer teaching, where all students act as teachers. These studies could be considered as deviant cases due to their scarcity (Ames et al., 2019), possibly this pedagogical practice is rare, primarily found in teacher education.

Conversely, studies of cross-level peer teaching replacing the teacher permanently are more common. While these studies might not yield much data on collective peer learning, they could offer valuable insights into the other two learning positions—peer student learning and peer teacher learning—providing a more comprehensive understanding of the interplay between all three learning dimensions. Although the review focuses on tertiary education studies, the sampling encompasses various educational contexts, extending beyond teacher education.

Because the emphasis is on synthesizing qualitative findings from empirical studies, it is not possible, nor necessary, to include as many relevant studies as possible (Thomas & Harden, 2008).

Choosing a limited number of studies offers a dual advantage—it allows for an in-depth analysis of each article and facilitates a meticulous comparison of various instructional designs (Ames et al., 2019; Thomas & Harden, 2008). The review aims to expand our understanding of this form of peer teaching by reorganizing empirical findings into new categories or themes (Ames et al., 2019).

This type of review underscores the importance of incorporating data-rich studies, as they typically offer profound insights into the topic under investigation, while also enabling novel interpretations (Ames et al., 2019). Qualitative studies are particularly valuable, providing a detailed account of learning processes within authentic educational settings.

Therefore, studies presenting significant qualitative data, such as quotations or excerpts, were prioritized during the selection process. However, the length of articles will often limit the number of available quotations, posing a challenge for qualitative data extraction. For instance, some of the data from the collective peer teaching studies were less abundant, but they were still deemed crucial for inclusion.

In the selection of cross-level peer teaching studies, it was easier to identify high-impact, data-rich studies. Furthermore, it should be noted that, given the scarcity of peer teaching studies relying solely on qualitative data, most included studies employ a mixed-methods approach, combining qualitative and quantitative research techniques.

Search methodology

Part of the challenge with "learning by teaching" as a research field, is that many different terms are used to describe similar pedagogical practices. Several teaching methods are relevant, but they have their own terms such as "reciprocal teaching," "cooperative learning" or the "jigsaw method." Different labels are also used to describe peer teaching, for example "peer learning" (Topping, 2005), "peer-assisted learning" (Topping & Ehly, 1998) and even "peer-to-peer teaching" (Stigmar, 2016). In the previous chapter, the conceptual relationship between "peer tutoring" and "peer teaching" was also clarified. In addition, there are a number of affiliated terms such as peer modeling (Schunk, 1998), peer monitoring (Henington & Skinner, 1998), peer mentoring, and peer assessment (Topping, 2009). Although these terms describe different learning activities, they all transfer some aspect of teaching behavior to the students.

The first search phase was performed in Google Scholar with keywords like "learning by teaching," "peer teaching," and "peer tutoring." A substantial effort was put into screening titles and abstracts to identify if they fulfilled the most important searching criterium: *formal peer teaching of the whole class*. The preliminary findings showed that many of the articles used quantitative research methods; especially experimental studies which were not relevant to include. These experimental studies typically examine one-to-one tutoring situations and aim to identify one or a few crucial cognitive factors that produce positive learning outcomes (Fiorella & Mayer, 2013; Kobayashi, 2021a; Roscoe & Chi, 2008). These studies do not involve peer teaching of a larger student group and they are also low on ecological validity. Especially the student motivation may be very different when students replace the teacher in front of the class in an authentic setting.

Concerning cross-level peer teaching, a large number of studies from different educational contexts were identified, often defined as peer tutoring. However, there are a lot fewer studies which use qualitative data. A "highly cited" (Cited by 507) study by Lockspeiser et al. (2008) in medical school was found to be particularly interesting. The instructional design let peer teachers be responsible for groups of 5–10 peer students in medical school, and the article presented detailed qualitative data. In addition, the notion of congruence is used as an interesting key term to explain the learning processes in peer teaching. By snowballing the references in this article, another interesting older study was identified (Moust & Schmidt, 1994). This is a highly cited study which also includes detailed qualitative data about student perceptions of the learning process. Only a few articles were identified which build on collective peer teaching by letting students rotate on being peer teachers for each other (Aslan, 2015, 2017a, 2017b). The qualitative data is primarily student perceptions of the learning process. Although the quality of these studies varies, all articles were included. Snowballing also led to the inclusion of one extra article on what could be labeled as collective peer teaching (Velez et al., 2011).

An overview of selected studies

In total, six studies were selected for the "qualitative systematic review." All studies involve formal peer teaching of the whole group. The instructional design allows peer teachers to replace the teacher in front of the class. Two studies build on "cross-level" peer teaching (Lockspeiser et al., 2008; Moust & Schmidt, 1994), while four studies describe "same-level" collective peer teaching which involve all students being teachers for each other (Aslan, 2015, 2017a, 2017b; Velez et al., 2011).

Second, all studies are from professional studies in tertiary education, including teacher education (Aslan, 2015, 2017a, 2017b; Velez et al., 2011), law (Moust & Schmidt, 1994), and medicine (Lockspeiser et al., 2008). By selecting studies from a wide variety of educational programs, the goal is to present commonalities across educational settings. However, all collective peer teaching studies are from teacher education, indicating that this pedagogical practice is most common in this educational context because of the importance of teacher training.

Third, all studies are relatively new except the study by Moust and Schmidt (1994) which is quite old. However, this is a highly cited paper and the qualitative data in the article include lengthy excerpts of the interview data.

Fourth, all studies examine student perceptions of the learning process. All studies include interview data, either individually or in groups. The cross-level peer teaching study by Lockspeiser et al. (2008) also include both interviews with both peer teachers and peer students. The peer tutors, here labeled as peer teachers, are students at a higher educational level, who have recently completed the course the students are attending. Both cross-level peer teaching studies are also interesting because they explicitly compare student perceptions of peer teaching with faculty teaching.

Fifth, it varies to what degree the qualitative data have been analyzed within a theoretical framework. In the studies by Aslan (2015, 2017a, 2017b), a lot of the qualitative data presented has been inductively coded and many of the quotations are presented with few additional comments or theoretical interpretations. In contrast, the qualitative data presented by Moust and Schmidt (1994) and Lockspeiser et al. (2008) are categorized in relation to a few general theoretical terms, such as congruence. Still, these studies include several lengthy quotations with relatively short interpretations or explanations.

Review analysis

This review primarily includes the empirical findings in the different articles, both quantitative and qualitative data. All of the data has been recategorized in relation to one of the three learning positions. In the first part of the review, each article has been analyzed separately, providing a detailed summary of how the findings are relevant for the different learning positions.

By selecting only a few articles in the review, it is also easier to move from a descriptive analysis to a more interpretive analysis. In some of the selected studies, fewer theoretical concepts are used and the authors "let participants speak for themselves" to a greater degree. It was relatively easy to identify and reuse quotations in these studies (Thomas & Harden, 2008). The aim is to provide more depth and richness when extracting the data, primarily student perceptions of all three learning positions. On the one hand, the maximum variation sampling strategy is useful for documenting uniqueness, but in addition it can be important in identifying shared patterns across cases and heterogeneity (Ames et al., 2019).

Therefore, it is important to "go beyond" the primary studies. A qualitative systematic review should be more than the sum of parts and offer novel interpretations. These cannot be found in just one single report but are inferences that build on all the selected studies (Thomas & Harden, 2008). The second phase of the analysis follows this strategy, by comparing all the recategorized empirical data with the aim of providing a more coherent description of the phenomenon. This analysis is performed in the summary section of the review chapter. Here, the most important commonalities and differences across the selected studies are identified in relation to the three learning positions. The goal is to establish a conceptual understanding based on the existing studies (Ames et al., 2019; Thomas & Harden, 2008). In all the succeeding chapters, involving both empirical analysis (Chapters 3 and 4) and theoretical analysis (Chapters 5, 6, and 7), the three learning positions will be analyzed and further discussed.

Article nr.1—Velez et al. (2011)

About the instructional design and the research study

The first selected article is titled "Cultivating change through peer teaching" (2011) and authored by J. J. Velez, J. Cano, M. S. Whittington, and K. J. Wolf. Velez et al. (2011) examine two "Introduction to Teaching" courses in agricultural and extension education. Because all students were required to engage in peer teaching activities, this instructional design has been labeled as a collective peer teaching design. In the research study, there were 23 students on the main campus and 16 students on the branch campus. The course content was the same, but each course had a different instructor. Collective peer teaching was conducted during the last five weeks of a ten-week course. The students were paired in groups of two or three (co-teaching) and assigned to teach a 50-minute class session. The subject matter had to build on one specific chapter of the course text, but the peer teachers were also encouraged to be creative in the use of teaching methods. In addition, all peer teachers had to provide a list of possible test questions over the material they taught. After the peer lesson, the peer teachers received feedback, 10 minutes from the peer students and 20 minutes from the formal teacher. The formal teacher both asked questions, clarified issues, and if necessary, gave additional explanations. Right after the class finished, the peer teachers also remained together with the formal teacher for a private 15-minute reflection on the lesson. A notable feature here is the substantial amount of time dedicated to feedback, with peers being encouraged to comment on anything about the lesson afterward (Velez et al., 2011).

The main purpose of the research study is to describe student perceptions of peer teaching and its impact on the classroom environment. The researchers did both observations, individual interviews, and focus groups, and used data triangulation (Velez et al., 2011). The findings have been organized according to the three learning positions.

Peer teacher learning

Regarding lesson preparations, the peer teachers found it difficult to identify "things that are important" and some needed guidance from the formal teacher. Therefore, they were given detailed notes on the subject matter in advance. Peer teachers report satisfaction with how the formal teacher provided guidance both before and immediately after the lesson.

Furthermore, the students became more aware of learning by teaching as a pedagogical practice. When they reflect on their own learning, they made statements such as "I'd rather teach than learn" and "I learn more when I teach" (Velez et al., 2011, p. 44). The peer teachers also became more aware on how they could improve both their teaching styles. Metacognition was supported through the feedback processes, resulting in peer teachers becoming more aware of both their individual learning style and how they worked together as a peer teacher group. For example, to make it easier to divide the teaching load, they recommended peer teacher groups of two as opposed to three (Velez et al., 2011).

Peer student learning

Regarding the peer student learning, the students gave a lot of verbal praise to the peer teachers, even though they felt the feedback time was too short. Regarding the quality of the peer lesson, some even remarked that the peer teaching was more interesting than the faculty teaching:

> ...that's what our instructors are there to do, to lecture, put the material out, let us learn it and then have an exam about it. It is pretty cut-and-dry, straightforward, here is the material. At least with this [peer teaching] we are doing more hands on, we get into groups, we do something to apply the knowledge that we just learned, it makes it more interesting to me.
> (Velez et al., 2011, p. 44)

Another student stated that this type of teaching was more relevant, "They could come up with examples more true to the times" (Velez et al., 2011, p. 45). Furthermore, the students experienced that this type of teaching created more student engagement. One student said: "Having students teach gives it a fresh outlook and a creative take on material" (Velez et al., 2011, p. 44). Another student claimed the formal teachers were too old and spoke a different language:

> I mean if they are like 140 and they are talking about something old school, and I don't really know what they are talking about and they are using it as an example, that's going to get in my way.
> (Velez et al., 2011, p. 45)

Collective peer learning

Regarding the collective peer learning, the researchers observed a positive change in the classroom dynamics with students appearing to be active and vibrant. The peer teachers engaged in the lessons with increased openness and comfort with their peers. The observers noticed that students and peer teachers engaged in "warm and interactive, joking personal interaction" (Velez et al., 2011, p. 45). One student stated that the class atmosphere during peer teaching was better: "it is lighter, it is more relaxed, you are not as tense and sitting there and having to hang on every word the professor says. It's like, hey that's my friend. You can talk to them easier" (Velez et al., 2011, p. 45). The students were also polite toward each other, and they were more forgiving of mistakes. Compared with instructor-led college courses, there was also more physical contact and verbal praise. This increased the sense of communality (Velez et al., 2011). Another peer student commented on how the whole-class discussions improved:

> I actually like it [peer teaching] because you feel like you are on the same level as everyone else. You don't feel like you are pressured to hide what you want to say, you can say anything and everyone wants to share; and, it is a change from having a professor sit there and lecture you, so I like it.
> (Velez et al., 2011, p. 45)

The discussions were experienced to be more symmetrical and open with everyone wanting to share their opinions. The students experienced greater freedom to candidly share their thoughts. The peer teachers effectively created a warm and interactive classroom environment, allowing more students to feel free from the relational constraints of the traditional instructor-centered setting (Velez et al., 2011).

Furthermore, all students were given the opportunity to take more risks in their teaching. At an aggregated level, the peer teachers also utilized diverse teaching methods, yet constantly focused on personal interaction and relational activities specific to their age group. The students also learned a lot about teaching by comparing the different peer lessons. However, peer teachers who had the first lessons felt they had a disadvantage because they could not get any ideas from others. One of them states:

> I know at least with our group, since we were the first ones to go we really felt like the guinea pigs because we weren't sure what to expect"; "It was a pretty obvious benefit for the other groups, the later groups, they hear the comments at the end from all the groups that have gone, on what to improve on.
>
> (Velez et al., 2011, p. 44)

Perceptions of unfairness increased because some peer teachers could learn more than others before they had their lesson. In conclusion, this study is interesting because the empirical findings cover all the three learning positions.

Article nr.2—Moust and Schmidt (1994)

The instructional design and the research study

The second selected article is titled "Facilitating small-group learning: a comparison of student and staff tutors' behavior" (1994) and authored by J. H. Moust and H. G. Schmidt. This study examines two eight-week courses in the first-year curriculum in an integrated problem-based law curriculum. All students attended small-group tutorials, normally with 11 students, twice a week for two hours. These groups were either guided by student tutors, here labeled as peer teachers, or staff tutors who are described as faculty teachers. The sessions built on problem-based learning which was the main instructional approach. Students had to work on various problems related to lawbreaking behavior. The students were introduced to carefully constructed problems and challenged to discuss these problems and produce tentative explanations for the phenomena. The teacher (tutor) would help students integrate and use information and avoid misinterpretations of the subject matter. Although the teacher could contribute with some direct teaching, the process primarily involved facilitation of the students' learning (Moust & Schmidt, 1994). Since this instructional approach is staff-intensive, it is common to hire advanced undergraduate students as teachers. This has raised the question of whether peer teacher groups perform as good as faculty-led groups.

In the present study, the two courses included approximately 350 students, with 22 faculty teachers and peer teachers. The peer teachers were cross-level, recruited openly among third- and fourth-year undergraduate students. They received the same preparation for the teacher role as the faculty staff. The data collection includes both interviews and a quantitative survey. After the course, a student from each of the 22 tutorial groups was interviewed. This facilitated a more systematic collection and comparison of opinions about the behavior of peer teachers and faculty teachers.

In the articles, several student quotes have also been included and analyzed. The teacher's performance was also measured by letting all students complete a 39-item Likert-type rating scale. The survey included items related to both the subject matter and the learning processes (Moust & Schmidt, 1994).

Peer student learning

In general, the quantitative survey finds that students perceive the peer teachers to be equally good as faculty teachers in most areas. Because faculty teachers have more knowledge on the subject matter, the peer teachers must bring in something else which is of pedagogical value, but the big question is what this can be. The article reveals several interesting findings related to what could be labeled as peer student learning. Some of these quotes have here been reanalyzed in more detail.

A stronger focus on assessment

Concerning learning of the subject matter, the survey shows that were few differences between faculty teachers and the peer teachers. However, there were significant differences in assessment orientation with peer teachers using the end-of-course exam more frequently to direct students' activities. In the interview, one student says:

> Student tutors also give you information about what you have to study for your exams. "That is a really relevant piece of information, you should know that, you should get a question about it," or: "That piece of information you will need often in the next years." Student tutors have that still fresh in their minds. And because they have that experience themselves, they are better able to transmit it to us. They are better able, in comparison to staff tutors, to give us examples of assessment. They know what is really important for the achievement test.
>
> (Moust & Schmidt, 1994, p. 297)

Here, the student emphasizes that the student tutors or peer teachers provide highly relevant information on how to prepare for the final exam. They have this knowledge "fresh in their minds" because they have just recently passed the course and been through the same experience. Although the student tutors have less academic background knowledge than the faculty tutors, the student says that they still provide better "examples of assessment." Statements such as "That is a really relevant piece of information, you should know that, you should get a question about it" suggest that they are more specific in the advice they give. They remember the challenges the students are facing, providing a student perspective on the assessment situation.

Another peer student remarks that the peer teacher gives them very relevant and specific information on how to prepare for the exam. The peer teachers mention what authors, arguments, and concepts to be evaluated positively. However, one can question if this help risks becoming "too strategic" by reducing it to a new type of knowledge telling. To a lesser degree, students will need to find out things by themselves. By only talking about the exam, one risks instrumentalizing the interest in the subject matter. Although student satisfaction is high, it may primarily be due to extrinsic grade motivation. On the other hand, some students may have a too high level of performance anxiety, especially in law studies where grades are often considered important for later professional work (Sander & Bambauer, 2012). In this context, a "teaching to the test" approach may relieve performance anxiety and improve students' learning strategies and self-confidence.

More cognitive congruence

The second element was labeled as "cognitive congruency" and examines to what degree peer teachers manage to understand the students and express themselves at their level of knowledge. In the survey, peer teachers were perceived to be better at understanding the nature of the problems students faced in attempting to master the subject matter. This includes the peer teacher asking questions we could understand, using the same terminology as we did and succeeding in explaining topics comprehensibly. These differences were significant and relatively large (Moust & Schmidt, 1994). In the interviews, the students also claimed that the student tutors had a better understanding of the nature of the problems. One student says:

> Well, I prefer a student tutor. Because they are much closer to the mind of the student. They see through our difficulties because they have already encountered them themselves. They are more involved with the subject matter. I think they see very clearly which difficulties you can have with certain aspects of a subject. Whether you are not able to discern the main directions or whether you do not understand the details.
> (Moust & Schmidt, 1994, p. 296)

In the phrase "closer to the mind of the student," a proximity is described that is very valuable for the learning process. This student mentions especially how the peer tutors can identify "difficulties," indicating a stronger focus on learning needs in relation to the subject matter. On the one hand, the phrase "main directions" suggests that it can involve more general aspects of the subject. On the other hand, it may also be necessary to clarify certain "details." According to this student, the tutors are "more involved with the subject matter," and they appear to be more engaged in the teaching. Obviously, faculty staff will possess more elaborated, more accurate, and more differentiated knowledge structures, but they are less like the first-year students. Therefore, the peer teacher might be better able to help the students master the subject matter because the explanations are at a more similar conceptual level. They both use a more similar language, and they are more able to link concepts, relationships, and facts (Moust & Schmidt, 1994).

Another student emphasizes how the peer teacher (tutor) was very motivated:

> I really enjoyed it, the way our (student) tutor was guiding the group. She was so motivated. I was curious to know Why she was so attentive. Frequently she remarked: "Yeah, as a first-year student I had trouble in understanding that literature myself. I got some grip on it by working so and so," or: "You have to be keen on those aspects, they are really important in the next year." She showed us her own route of learning, her own problems with the learning materials and the way she tried to solve them. She also told us a lot about her own experiences with problem-based learning.
> (Moust & Schmidt, 1994, p. 297)

Here, the peer teacher (tutor) models the problem-solving process by describing "her own route of learning" and "her own problems with the learning materials." This includes recommendations on what literature is important to read and how she solved different problems. The students can identify with teachers who have also struggled to understand the subject matter. Obviously, a faculty teacher will not remember this experience in an equally vivid way. From the student perspective, it is an advantage that the peer teacher is more like the students. For example, another student remarks,

> She (a student tutor) understood exactly the problems we were struggling with at certain moments. Other tutors said after a while "Oh, now I understand what your problem is, well, that can be explained so and so" but she was mostly able to say in one word what our difficulties were.'
> (Moust & Schmidt, 1994, p. 296)

The phrase "say in one word what our difficulties were" suggests that the peer tutor was able to use a language that the students more easily understood. The phrase "understood exactly the problems we were struggling with" also indicates that there is a greater understanding of the difficulties the student have. The faculty teachers are less capable of imagining the learning problems students face (Moust & Schmidt, 1994).

Being more personal

Three elements or categories were also included in the process-facilitation component. One category described to what extent a peer teacher was interested in how the student group cooperated. Other studies have shown that students communicate more freely with each other when faculty staff are absent. In this survey, there were no differences between peer teacher and faculty teachers. Authority was a second category that described to what extent a peer teacher exercised his or her power to direct students' activities in the group. Here, faculty teachers showed more authoritarian behavior than peer teachers. A third category was "role congruency" which described to what extent a peer teacher was able to empathize with and relate to students' life experience. Here, the empirical findings show that peer tutors were more interested in students' daily lives, study experiences, and personalities. The statistical differences were significant and relatively large. The students also experienced the peer teacher as very engaged with the student (Moust & Schmidt, 1994). For example, one student states:

> Student tutors know what you have to do, how a small tutorial group has to perform. They are educated in problem-based learning. They have grown up with this approach. They know what a student needs from his or her tutor. And …. I am often disappointed by staff tutors. The staff tutor I had in the last course was not really interested. Whether you were present or not, whether you were engaged or not. (S)he was not engaged. Whereas student tutors show involvement by saying "Come on, you have to be here. These are really important materials. We will master it together. And if you have any trouble, you can come to me." If you are that close, that is much more pleasant. Then you feel much more motivated to get your teeth into the stuff.
> (Moust & Schmidt, 1994, p. 297)

Here, the student emphasizes that the peer teacher (student tutor) knows what "a student needs." They are much more engaged in the students and make suggestion on what is "really important materials." They explicitly say that they want the students to attend the lessons and show sincere interest in the students' learning process. They are curious about how the students experience the learning environment and other personal difficulties they face. Another advantage is that they "speak the language of the students." In contrast, faculty teachers are often not really interested in the students (Moust & Schmidt, 1994).

Article nr.3—Lockspeiser et al. (2008)

The instructional design and the research study

The third selected article is titled "Understanding the experience of being taught by peers: the value of social and cognitive congruence" (2008) and authored by T. M. Lockspeiser, P. O'Sullivan, A. Teherani, and J. Muller. Most medical schools have peer tutoring or cross-level peer teaching programs. This study examines how first- and second-year medical students perceived being part of a supplemental peer teaching program involving 141 students at the University of California. During the first six months of medical school, several second-year medical students functioned as cross-level peer teachers by facilitating weekly review sessions in anatomy and major organ systems. These sessions or lessons were organized four times each week with groups of 5–10 peer students, and the peer students would receive credits if they chose to participate (Lockspeiser et al., 2008).

The research study includes focus-group interviews with both first-year peer students and second-year peer teachers. These interviews were also used to design a questionnaire that was administered to 110 first-year students at the end of the year. In the original article, the qualitative data include some quotations from the interviews, which provide more detailed insights into the learning process. The theoretical framework builds loosely on the terms cognitive or social congruence. Here, the empirical findings are recategorized according to the three learning positions: peer student learning, peer teacher learning, and collective learning.

Peer student learning

More relevant teaching

Regarding peer student learning, the students perceived that the peer teachers made the lessons relevant. The highest rated item in the survey refers to peer teachers approaching the subject matter in a useful way. Here, several factors are of importance.

First, the peer teachers were able to review the material. This is important because many first-year students experienced it as very challenging to get an overview of the subject matter in their courses. In this context, the peer teaching lessons were important, as one student explains how these lessons were helpful:

> When we were doing endocarditis and myocarditis and all that, I had no idea how they all related to each other. And MSP (read: "peer teachers") did a really good job of connecting all the different lectures done by different people.
>
> (Lockspeiser et al., 2008, p. 366)

The peer teacher helped connect the various concepts taught in the course and organize all the information in a concise way (Lockspeiser et al., 2008).

Second, they can provide alternate explanations of concepts, helping them to integrate the individual concepts in the course. When comparing the peer teaching with faculty, some highlight that they are better cognitive matches.

For example, one student says, "The thing with peer teaching is that because they're not experts, they have a better understanding of what the basics are. When you're an expert like the faculty what you think is basic is no longer basic" (Lockspeiser et al., 2008, p. 365). Because the peer teachers have recently learned the material themselves, they are able to teach at an appropriate level. This also involves simple explanations of basic concepts. Opposite, the problem with the faculty teacher is that too much background knowledge makes it difficult to use a language that is easy to understand (Lockspeiser et al., 2008).

Third, the peer teachers share their own learning experiences and approaches to the academic content. For example, one student remarked about the second-year peer teachers, "They have the perspective of having just learned it as opposed to innately knowing it and ... they remember recently having gone through the learning process" (Lockspeiser et al., 2008, p. 365). Because the peer teachers have their own problem-solving process fresh in memory, they can describe it in detail and share the most relevant learning experiences. The peer teachers were more able to anticipate what problems the first-year students would meet when learning concepts. They can explain why a concept is difficult to learn and how they had managed to overcome their academic challenges (Lockspeiser et al., 2008).

Model learning

Furthermore, students are keen observers of their peer teachers. A first-year medical student comments on the experience of observing second-year peer teachers:

> I felt like watching the second-years and the way they handled just the tools and how they handled the bodies in general really gave me an idea of how to handle the body myself... the ease with which they were using things and not afraid of everything—that was kind of comforting.
> (Lockspeiser et al., 2008, p. 366)

The comment suggests that students pay closer attention to details in the teacher behavior than in traditional faculty teaching. The intensity of the observation appears to be stronger because students are aware that they can develop the same level of skills or knowledge. In the same study, another student reports that observing others increased their self-confidence, "Just the confidence of knowing that the second-years made it, they're still alive, they know this, I can do it too" (Lockspeiser et al., 2008, p. 366). Peer teachers who have recently completed a course manifest what success looks like. Conversely, students may identify less with a professional faculty teacher because they do not expect to reach the same level of expertise.

Improved emotional support to the students

Furthermore, peer teachers provided good emotional support to the students. For instance, one student explains how the peer teachers reduced fears and anxiety about medical school: "We know this material is tough. It's the first month of med school, relax, it's gonna be okay, it's not as bad as it really seems" (Lockspeiser et al., 2008, p. 365). The second-year peer teachers helped normalize the experience of being a first-year medical student by reducing the performance anxiety and gain trust in their own learning. They also showed empathy in expressing an understanding of how hard the learning process was (Lockspeiser et al., 2008).

More engaging teaching

Fourth, the peer teaching was more engaging because the peer teachers used different teaching styles than the faculty teachers. One student remarked: "I think [the MSP peer teachers] were more comfortable with kind of dumbing things down and just teaching it in a simpler way, and making silly mnemonics and things that I don't think the faculty would do" (Lockspeiser et al., 2008, p. 366). Another student said, "I'm an interactive learner, I remember things when people quiz me on them … MSP [the peer teachers] does that, lectures don't" (Lockspeiser et al., 2008, p. 367). The first-year students found the alternative teaching methods like the use of mnemonics to be both helpful and fun. Compared with the lecturers, the peer teachers used both more visual teaching methods and interactive methods such as quizzes.

Peer teacher learning

Regarding peer teacher learning, some expressed that they valued the opportunity to review and relearn material from the first year. Others were motivated by the social responsibility for others. One peer teacher stated, "I was motivated to learn at a deeper level because I was more motivated to learn for them than I was for myself" (Lockspeiser et al., 2008, p. 367). Here, the peer teacher suggests that there is a link between deep learning and being responsible for others learning. In addition, the peer teachers also express a need for more teacher training to improve their lessons (Lockspeiser et al., 2008).

Collective peer learning

Regarding collective peer learning, some peer teachers highlight the feeling of communality. For example, one peer teacher remarked, "I got a sense of fulfillment from teaching MSP. It was great to be able to help others with things that were not easy for me in first-year but that I finally understood" (Lockspeiser et al., 2008, p. 367). This peer teacher expresses "a sense of fulfillment from teaching," indicating a deep and personal motivation when being able to help other students with difficult academic topics. The peer teachers also enjoyed giving something back to the medical school community. The peer teaching also stimulated contact and informal support within and between the different medical school classes.

Article nr.4—Aslan (2015)

The instructional design and the research study

The fourth selected article is titled "Is learning by teaching effective in gaining 21st century skills? The views of pre-service science teachers" (2015) and authored by S. Aslan. The research study examines how these student teachers perceive learning-by-teaching as a pedagogical practice in a science education context and how it can support the development of 21st-century skills, such as life and career skills, learning and innovation skills, and digital literacy skills (Aslan, 2015).

The data has been collected from a Special Topics in Chemistry course in science teacher education in Turkey. This course aims to strengthen the understanding of the relationship between social and technological change as well as transformations in science and the natural environment. In this collective peer teaching, all students had to be teachers for the whole class. They were organized in small peer teacher groups with four or five students who had responsibility for one of the weekly lessons. In preparing the lesson, students had to do their own research and transform this information into a relevant lesson. The groups could freely choose a topic according to their preference and the teaching methods they wanted to use. For instance, one student group mapped why citizens used tap water or bottled water and what the reasons were for their choice. Before they started, the students also received information about peer teaching as a pedagogical practice. In addition, the students had to make a video or PowerPoint presentation which addressed the research question and write a letter that summarized what they had learned (Aslan, 2015).

Two pilot studies were conducted to refine the collective peer teaching design in 2012 and 2013. The final course design covered nine topics over a period of 12 weeks during the autumn of 2014. There were 43 student teachers in the course, but only those 33 students who regularly attended the lessons were included in the study. This includes 10 male and 23 female students between the age of 19 and 21 (Aslan, 2015).

The qualitative case study collected data by using a questionnaire (written interview) with 11 open-ended questions and a focus-group interview with one person from each of the seven peer teacher groups. This article presents a lot of data, often as quotations without any further interpretations. The primary focus is to rank student statements according to how frequently they appear. Here, several of these quotations will be analyzed in relation to the three different learning positions.[3]

Peer teacher learning

Regarding peer teacher learning, several students state how the peer teaching have made them think differently about how learning happens. For example, one student says, "I now realize that full learning happens when you teach the things you know to others" (Aslan, 2015, p. 1448). In this statement, the student acknowledges teaching as the most powerful type of learning. It illustrates that entering the role of peer teacher can potentially lead to fundamental change in student views of how learning happens. The phrase "full learning" indicates that deep learning has happened. Furthermore, several students highlight that much of the learning happens in the lesson preparations. However, some found it difficult to transform the science topics into relevant lesson content. For example, one student commented: "To me, it was difficult to simplify the subject according to the level of the students. I asked myself, 'Can I simplify this? Is it comprehensible'" (Aslan, 2015, p. 1451). The student found it difficult to summarize and simplify the topic in a meaningful way. It illustrates the need to have realistic expectations concerning what understanding students can acquire. Another disadvantage was that some students reported that they did not focus on other topics than the one they were responsible for.

Moreover, some students highlight how peer teacher collaboration could improve the quality of the lesson. One student remarked:

> Learning different ideas and creating something with different ideas was very enjoyable. One idea is not enough. For example, we were a group of five people. Five ideas emerged and we evaluated these five ideas, taking in its essence. In my opinion, it is very beautiful and valuable.
>
> (Aslan, 2015, p. 1448)

In this case, the group was able to both harness a diversity of ideas assess them and combine them into a better solution. However, Aslan (2015) finds that a major disadvantage is that several peer teacher groups struggled in their collaboration. The groups found it difficult to coordinate their preparations and reach an agreement on what to do. This may have become more difficult since the groups were as large as four to five students and there was little time to prepare the lesson and short deadlines. For example, one student stated, "Poor preparation leads to misconceptions" (Aslan, 2015, p. 1451). Part of the problem was also that some of the students were not so interested in the peer teaching. Some peer teacher groups also found it difficult to meet and there were even personal conflicts in some of the groups (Aslan, 2015).

In general, 91% (30 of 33) students were positive to *learning by teaching being used as a teaching method* in teacher education (Aslan, 2015). Several students expressed positive emotions because it provided them with relevant teaching experience. For example, one student commented, "It helps to facilitate learning. It also helps us be more qualified teachers for the future" (Aslan, 2015, p. 1451). A majority of students mentioned how it strengthened their vocational competence (54%). Some students underline how they became more conscious about their teaching behavior. One student commented, "I have seen my inadequacies and I will be more careful" (Aslan, 2015, p. 1453). Others mention improvement in classroom management and communication, like one student who learned to be careful about not talking too fast. Others mention the importance of lesson preparations.

In addition, some students mentioned the importance of improving their self-confidence as teachers. One student said: "It helps in development of self-confidence. It helps by gaining experiences associated with the teaching profession and in overcoming the fear of being a teacher" (Aslan, 2015, p. 1451). Although most students were joyful about being peer teachers, several also struggled to control their nervousness. One student stated:

> I got too nervous, thus, I found it difficult to express myself. It was difficult for me, but it helped me to think that I could suppress my nervousness. Of course, the process was important at the same time. Having the instructor there helped me to suppress my nervousness in time.
>
> (Aslan, 2015, p. 1452)

This statement illustrates that the performance anxiety in some cases appears to have had a negative influence on the quality of the peer teaching.

Collective peer learning

In the article, there is little focus on collective peer learning. However, the nervousness that some experienced when standing in front of the class may be related to a less than optimal class atmosphere. For example, one student says, "While maintaining the lesson, I managed to be less nervous and more comfortable. I could make eye contact. It was very important for me" (Aslan, 2015, p. 1447). Some peer teachers felt they lacked authority in the classroom and that other peer students did not take the lesson seriously. It indicates that the learning environment was not ideal (Aslan, 2015).

Peer student learning

Regarding the peer student learning, there were several challenges. Half of the students mentioned that peer students had difficulties getting the attention of students and involving them in the lesson. They struggled to maintain discipline in class. In addition, the students considered misconceptions to be a major weakness with this type of teaching, especially when some of the peer teachers were not sufficiently prepared (Aslan, 2015). Aslan (2015) claims the formal teacher can provide key support by helping students realize mistakes or misconceptions, provide alternative ideas, support lesson preparations, and strengthen student self-confidence and motivation.

Article nr.5—Aslan (2017a)

The instructional design and the research study

The fifth selected article is titled "The effect of learning by teaching on pre-service science teachers' attitudes towards chemistry" (2017a) and authored by S. Aslan. This study aims to understand the effect of learning by teaching on pre-service science teachers' attitudes toward chemistry. Like in the article by Aslan (2015), the course covers Special Topics in Chemistry at the science education program at a university in Turkey. It involves 11 different topics that all address the relationship between science, technology, society, and environment (STSE). One of the course objectives is to develop a more positive attitude toward chemistry. The instructional design builds on collective peer teaching (Aslan, 2017a).

The data collection was done in the autumn of 2015. Forty-nine pre-service science teachers participated: ranging in age from 19 to 22, including both females (n = 31) and males (n = 18). Quantitative data was collected using a Chemistry Attitude Scale, which measured the effect of pre-service science teachers' attitudes toward chemistry using a pre-post measure. The scale includes 15 items placed on a five-point Likert scale (Aslan, 2017a). In addition, 11 individual interviews were done with one member from each group of peer co-teachers. These interviews mapped how the peer teaching design influenced the student teachers' attitudes toward chemistry.

Peer teacher learning

In general, the empirical findings in this article are directed toward peer teacher learning as a learning position. Only statements that were explicitly directed toward peer teaching have been included in this summary. Concerning the quantitative results, the course had a positive effect on pre-service science teachers' attitudes toward chemistry (Aslan, 2017a). The qualitative data provide more insight into how the students developed a stronger interest in chemistry, and how the subject matter became more meaningful. One student remarked: "I developed a new perspective. While I was teaching the chemistry content to my classmates, I felt that chemistry is very valuable. I think that making an effort to teach to my friends made it more valuable for us" (Aslan, 2017a, p. 10). It is interesting that the "effort to teach my friends" is what transforms the attitude. One explanation may be that it is usually expected that a teacher models an interest in the subject matter. By being given the responsibility to be a teacher, a positive interest in the subject matter is expected even if this is not the case. Another student also highlights a similar change of attitude: "If we carried on our lessons in the traditional way where we didn't have this kind of responsibility, I would never realize how enjoyable chemistry is. I noticed that chemistry is not boring at all, it is very enjoyable" (Aslan, 2017a, p. 10). This student highlights how the peer teacher role is superior in developing an interest in the subject matter. The statement also illustrates how students develop feelings toward the subject matter, both negative and positive. The transformation toward more positive feelings may have a very important long-term impact on the students' motivation to learn and teach chemistry in the future.

Article nr.6—Aslan (2017b)

The instructional design and the research study

The sixth selected article is titled "Learning by teaching: can it be utilized to develop inquiry skills?" (2017b) and authored by S. Aslan. This research study aims to investigate the effect of learning by teaching on student teachers inquiry skills. Like in the two other studies by Aslan (2015, 2017a), it builds on collective peer teaching and the course is Special Topics in Chemistry. The study was done in the autumn of 2016 and included 47 student teachers: 11 male and 36 female prospective teachers between 20 and 24 years old (Aslan, 2017b).

Both quantitative and qualitative research methods were used. The quantitative data was collected by using an "Inquiry Skills Scale" and a pre- and post-test in which the average points were compared with each other (t-test). The 14 items consisted of three dimensions: acquisition of information, control of information, and self-confidence (Aslan, 2017b). In the second phase, qualitative data was collected to get a more detailed understanding of how the pedagogical practice influenced the inquiry skills. These data were collective with a questionnaire (a structured interview form) with two questions. The first question was: "Do you think that learning by teaching has an impact on your inquiry skills?" The second question asked the informants to explain how learning by teaching influenced their inquiry skills (Aslan, 2017b).

In the article, Aslan used content analysis to analyze the data (Patton, 2014, p. 453). However, there are major methodological issues regarding the concept validity. When students refer to their perceptions of learning by teaching, they often primarily talk about the project work which was part of the lesson preparations. The quantitative data show that learning by teaching has a positive effect on the prospective science teachers' inquiry skills. There were statistically significant differences between the pre-test and post-test. A large majority of the students (41 of 46 students) also stated that the teaching method had a positive influence on the development of their inquiry skill (Aslan, 2017b). The weakness in the analysis is most of the quotations in the article are directed toward critical thinking and the use of multiple sources, which are typical features in project work. It indicates that students are instead referring to the benefits of inquiry learning, not peer teaching as a pedagogical practice. Therefore, student statements that address general aspects of inquiry learning have been left out.

Peer teacher learning

Still, there are some student statements that explicitly address peer teaching, and which are relevant in the analysis of the three learning positions. Regarding the peer teacher learning, several students highlight how it improved the student motivation. They mention the social obligation to acquire a deep understanding of the subject matter. One student commented, "I searched the subject fully and comprehended the parts that I hadn't understood so that I could explain them to others in the class in case they didn't understand either" (Aslan, 2017b, p. 194). In the role of teacher, there is a social obligation to understand the subject because other people depend on you. Another student says, "I had the opportunity to learn subjects permanently by searching about them and teaching what I learned instead of memorizing them. I think this boosted my motivation to learn" (Aslan, 2017b, p. 194). The phrase "learn subject permanently" indicates the presence of a deeper kind of learning. A hird student highlights a change in learning strategy from simple memorizing before the exam to a reading process that is about meaning-making. In preparing a lesson, the peer teachers are forced to prioritize and ensure that the lesson content is worth teaching. Another student also mentioned how this process improved the self-confidence.

Summary of the review

This review aims to provide a preliminary understanding of the complexity of the learning processes in formal peer teaching of the whole class. The analysis builds primarily on student perceptions and display a wide variety of interesting empirical findings that have been categorized according to the three learning positions: (1) Peer student learning, (2) Peer teacher learning, and (3) Collective peer learning. Table 2.1 provides an overview of learning positions described in the different articles.

In this summary, each learning position will be reviewed separately by comparing key empirical findings in the different articles.

34 Qualitative review—formal peer teaching of the whole group

Table 2.1 Overview of the three learning positions identified in the review

	1. Peer teacher learning	2. Peer student learning	3. Collective peer learning
Article nr.1: Velez et al. (2011)	X	X	X
Article nr.2: Moust and Schmidt (1994)		X	
Article nr.3: Lockspeiser et al. (2008)	X	X	X
Article nr.4: Aslan (2015)	X	X	X
Article nr.5: Aslan (2017a)	X		
Article nr.6: Aslan (2017b)	X		

Review of peer teacher learning

Regarding the peer teacher learning position, most of the studies in the review provide findings on how students perceived this type of learning (Aslan, 2015, 2017b; Lockspeiser et al., 2008; Velez et al., 2011). In this summary, some of the key characteristics are summarized.

First, the studies in the review show a *strong peer teacher motivation*, both for cross-level peer teachers (Lockspeiser et al., 2008; Moust & Schmidt, 1994) and same-level peer teachers (Aslan, 2015, 2017b). The special characteristic with this motivation is that it builds on a social commitment to help others. In order to teach what is important to others, one needs to acquire a deep understanding the subject matter (Aslan, 2017b; Lockspeiser et al., 2008). On the one hand, if the lesson is a success, peer teachers feel a strong sense of fulfillment (Lockspeiser et al., 2008). On the other hand, some peer teachers also report of performance anxiety and discomfort. For example, Aslan (2015) finds that student perceptions are mixed. While some students gain self-confidence and thrive on coping the performance anxiety, others report of a nervousness that appears to be too high. Although nearly all students in the study are positive, we still know little about motivation in a collective peer teaching design that involves all students. Several factors may influence the performance anxiety such as the degree of guidance, teacher training or background knowledge on the subject matter. In teacher education, this type of instructional design is extra relevant because of how it can support the development of teaching skills. In other educational programs, this argument will be less relevant.

Second, peer teachers can develop *more positive attitudes toward the subject matter*. In the study by Aslan (2017a), some of the comments indicate a transformational impact that move students from being negative or indifferent to strongly positive feelings toward chemistry. However, the disadvantage is that deep learning of one topic results in less comprehensive learning (Aslan, 2015). On the other hand, an attitudinal change toward the subject matter may be much more important for future learning and interest in the subject matter.

Third, peer teacher learning can *improve students learning strategies*. For example, in the study by Aslan (2017b), a student mentions that it is not enough to use simple repetition strategies in the lesson preparations. In one study, students had to strengthen their inquiry skills in preparing a lesson. It is not enough with simple repetition strategies (Aslan, 2017b). Two studies also highlight summarizing as a strategy in describing how peer teachers had to work hard to identify and select the most relevant lesson content (Aslan, 2015; Velez et al., 2011). Since this work is difficult, teacher guidance may be required. Students also become more aware of the different learning strategies they use when they prepare a lesson and discuss it with their peers and the formal teacher (Velez et al., 2011). Some students have even reconsidered their views on how they think learning and teaching happens by becoming more aware of learning by teaching as a pedagogical practice (Aslan, 2015).

Fourth, some studies emphasize how students *develop their teaching skills* (Aslan, 2015). This is particularly important in teacher education. On the one hand, this may involve training of microteaching skills such as presentation technique, communication skill, or classroom management. In addition, On the other hand, peer teaching can develop students' self-confidence if they are able to overcome their nervousness and collaborative difficulties in the peer teacher teams (Aslan, 2015).

Review of peer student learning

How do the articles describe peer student learning? Are there any characteristics that appear to differ from ordinary teaching? Several articles examine how student learning is similar or different to faculty teaching. An important question is how much more academic background knowledge a teacher needs? While "cross-level" peer teachers have significantly more background knowledge than their students, they have significantly less knowledge than a faculty teacher. Still peer students often think they have sufficient background knowledge and are able to teach it in a relevant way (Lockspeiser et al., 2008; Moust & Schmidt, 1994).

First, concerning *the subject matter* in the peer lessons, it appears to be more connected *to students' learning process*. For example, peer teachers enliven the subject matter by bringing in their own history of learning (Lockspeiser et al., 2008; Moust & Schmidt, 1994). Because peer teachers have the learning process fresh in their memory, it will typically be emotionally stronger and easier to articulate in more detail. In contrast, a faculty teacher would usually not remember this learning process as vividly. They can also provide more relevant examples and speak an academic language that students can easier understand (Lockspeiser et al., 2008; Velez et al., 2011).

Therefore, peer student learning will typically be more orientated toward *the learning needs of the students*. Peer teachers will often be more familiar with the problems students face because they have just recently gone through the same process (Lockspeiser et al., 2008; Moust & Schmidt, 1994). In contrast, some faculty teachers may also show very little interest in the students

(Moust & Schmidt, 1994). The personal approach to the teaching depends on the peer teaching design and will not always be present (Aslan, 2015). On the other hand, peer teaching risks reducing the level of academic learning due to potential misinterpretations and misconceptions (Aslan, 2015). To ensure high quality, several studies recommend preparation time with guidance from the formal teacher (Aslan, 2015; Velez et al., 2011).

Second, peer student learning emphasizes *exam preparations*. For example, in one study in the review, cross-level peer teachers referred to end-of-course examinations more frequently than faculty teachers (Moust & Schmidt, 1994). In contrast to a faculty teacher, a cross-level peer teacher will just recently also have completed the exam. This experience can be used to provide a relevant overview of the most important content (Lockspeiser et al., 2008) or help connect different concepts that are important for the final exam in the course (Moust & Schmidt, 1994). Because most students will usually be concerned about the exam, peer teachers often tend to have a stronger focus on "teaching to the test" than faculty teachers. In same-level peer teaching, the teaching itself will not necessarily be part of the formal assessment, but there can be additional written assignments that are relevant for the exam (Aslan, 2015).

Third, peer teachers show *more interest in the student as a person*, including their daily lives, student experiences, and personalities. They are often able to show better emotional support and empathy toward the students because they have had similar feelings or been in familiar situations. By belonging to the same age group, they establish a rapport with the peer students which the faculty teacher is usually not capable of (Lockspeiser et al., 2008; Moust & Schmidt, 1994). This was different in one of the studies of collective peer teaching where some of the peer teachers lacked interest in the teaching and the students (Aslan, 2015).

Fourth, several of the studies in the review find that peer teaching is *more engaging and fun* (Lockspeiser et al., 2008; Moust & Schmidt, 1994). One study shows that peer teachers also serve as powerful role models in displaying enthusiasm for the learning process (Moust & Schmidt, 1994). To the peer student, they manifest what is achievable within a short time frame. In same-level collective peer teaching, the results are more mixed. One study finds that students became more involved in the lessons (Velez et al., 2011), while another study reported that some students found that the peer teaching was boring (Aslan, 2015). In this case, one explanation may have been the peer teachers were young and inexperienced.

Review of collective peer learning

There were few data in the review that could be related to collective peer learning. One explanation is that this learning position will primarily be present in studies of collective peer teaching. Still, there were a few empirical findings.

First, there are examples of how students develop a *culture of sharing* by letting students do extra written assignments which they shared with the rest of the class in different ways. In one study, all peer teachers had to create summaries of their topics in the course (Aslan, 2015). In another study, they had to make a list of relevant exam question which was later used in the final assessment (Velez et al., 2011). This instructional design is very different from the cross-level peer teaching studies where only a few peer teachers are responsible for the lesson content (Moust & Schmidt, 1994)

Second, collective peer learning seeks to strengthen the *community of learners*. For example, in one study, the peer teacher experienced that they gave something back to the educational community (Lockspeiser et al., 2008). In another study, the researchers found a stronger sense of communality and increased sense of belonging. The setting was relaxed and involved more physical contact between the students, making it easier to talk. Students laughed and talked to each other throughout the lessons, creating a warm and inclusive atmosphere. More students were stimulated to engage in the classroom discussions. It was a class atmosphere with more symmetrical relations, different from the typical constraints that follow instructor interaction (Velez et al., 2011). However, some studies also show that students may experience the class atmosphere or learning environment as less safe (Aslan, 2015). A supportive class culture appears to be essential in reducing feeling of performance anxiety (Lockspeiser et al., 2008).

Third, some studies show that the peer teacher appreciated the *evaluative feedback* they got from their peers and the formal teacher. The students also learned by observing and discussing a variety of different lessons. These discussions stimulated reflections on the lessons, although the time was limited (Velez et al., 2011).

Fourth, several of the studies organize the students in peer teacher groups who *co-taught* the rest of the student group (Aslan, 2015; Velez et al., 2011). In one study, two or three peer teachers collaborated (Velez et al., 2011), while in the study by Aslan (2015), five students were together in doing a project and a lesson together. Although some groups found it difficult to collaborate in such a large group, some had a positive experience because of the diversity of ideas that were produced.

How will this review be used?

The main purpose of this review has been to identify what we already know about how learning emerges in formal peer teaching of the whole class. *Regarding peer student learning*, the review shows how the subject matter is more integrated into the students' learning process. The peer teachers remember the learning process better because they have just recently completed it. In their teaching, they both focus on exam preparations and show more interest in the student. In addition, peer teaching can be perceived as more engaging and fun. In *peer teacher learning*, the studies reveal a strong motivation to learn because of the social commitment to help others. In this role, peer teachers can also develop more positive attitudes toward the subject matter and improve their learning strategies. In addition, they can improve their teaching skills. Moreover, *collective peer learning* addresses students shared responsibility and how they can share lesson content, engage in whole-class discussions and evaluative feedback. Same-level collective peer teaching can also improve the class atmosphere.

Although there is no "conceptual saturation" of what characterizes the three learning positions (Ames et al., 2019; Thomas & Harden, 2008), the review still identifies several mechanisms that are relevant for further analysis. In Chapters 3 and 4, two case studies will be presented which build on collective peer teaching. These studies are analyzed according to these three learning positions and will expand on the findings from this review. In Chapters 5, 6, and 7, the findings of the two case studies will be compared with each other, and the learning positions will be discussed in relation to broader theoretical perspectives.

Notes

1 Qualitative evidence synthesis is another term that is used to describe a systematic review of qualitative research. There are also a number of similar types of review that are labeled in other ways, such as meta-ethnography "meta-study," "critical interpretive synthesis," and "metasynthesis." Thomas, J., & Harden, A. (2008). Methods for the thematic synthesis of qualitative research in systematic reviews. *BMC Medical Research Methodology, 8*, 45–45. https://doi.org/10.1186/1471-2288-8-45.
2 See Table 1.1 in Chapter 1 for an overview of the different types of peer teaching.
3 Note that there is some uncertainty regarding the concept validity of many of the qualitative statements. It is not always clear if the students are referring to the student project they did before the lesson or the actual peer teaching lesson. Statements that highlight the research project have been left out. This is an issue in all the articles published by Aslan in this review.

3 First case study—collective peer teaching in teacher education

The collective peer teaching design

The first case study is about a collective peer teaching design organized as a part of the Practical Pedagogical Education (PPU), one of the largest teacher education programs in Norway. This one-year program is offered to student teachers who have already completed a bachelor's degree in relevant school subjects. It qualifies for work in upper primary school, secondary school (grades 5–13 in the Norwegian school system), and adult education. The complete program includes two six-week school-placement periods and mandatory lessons in pedagogy and subject didactics on campus. The pedagogy classes cover topics such as theories of learning, human development, design of teaching, curriculum theory, and classroom management.

In this case study, the informants are part-time student teachers who follow the course over a two-year period. The data were collected in April 2019, at the end of the students' first year. The students had completed their first placement period and attended 21 days of teaching on campus, which comprised 15 days of pedagogy and six days of subject didactics. In pedagogy classes, the first year of teaching had primarily consisted of large-scale lectures with 80–90 students. All students had also completed a mandatory oral presentation of a pedagogical topic related to the school-placement period.

This study examines a peer teaching event that lasted two days and was part of the formal assessment. In the program, students are required to pass a midway test after the first year. Previously, this test had been organized as a traditional written exam, but now it was instead redesigned as a mandatory peer teaching assignment. Groups of two or three students were each given the responsibility for a 25-minute lesson. Each group of co-teachers could freely choose one of 40 predefined topics from the syllabus in pedagogy. They received information about the assignment approximately one month in advance. The students were also required to involve the rest of the class in bidirectional communication and active learning processes; it was not enough simply to lecture on the topic. By allowing students to teach each other, a strong emphasis was placed on practical teacher training in the assessment situation on campus.

All students were required to be teachers for the rest of the class. In total, 90 student teachers completed the first year of the program. However, 16 of them lived very far away from campus and were given the opportunity to do an alternative online assignment instead. Each student produced an instructional video and gave feedback to some of the other students.

At campus, 74 student teachers were involved in the collective peer teaching. In total, these students organized 28 lessons for two days. The whole student group was divided into two separate tracks, with approximately 20 students in each class. The lessons would take place in ordinary classrooms. During these two days, all students would also participate in a half-day workshop on body language. Therefore, every student followed ten different peer teaching lessons over one and a half days.

Moreover, because the lesson was relatively short, the students were compelled to identify the most important issues from the subject matter. All student groups also produced a written summary (around 1,000 words) of the subject matter, which was shared online with the whole class. These summaries could later be used as resources in preparing for the final oral exam.

Besides this, peer feedback was part of the design. The peer students had five minutes to give verbal feedback immediately after each lesson. In addition, anyone could give written anonymous feedback through an online questionnaire.

Concerning the formal assessment, the peer teaching performance was not graded by the teacher. Students only had to pass and would be given a second chance if they failed. A teacher educator was present during the lessons and offered brief comments immediately afterward. In addition, the students later received more detailed written feedback on their teaching performance and information on whether they had passed or not. While all students passed the practical peer teaching assignment, some groups were required to improve their written summaries.

The research study

In the first case study, an online survey was used to map how the student teachers perceived their participation in the peer teaching. All students were invited to respond to a questionnaire, which was sent out a few days after completion of the peer teaching assignment. Of the 74 students required to meet on campus, 58 completed the questionnaire, yielding a response rate of 78%. In this group, 35% of the students were male, and 65% were female. Although the students had a wide range of subject backgrounds, social science was by far the dominant subject background. A majority of the students also had significant teaching experience: 35% had several years, 35% had 1–2 years, and 31% had no experience.

The questionnaire was used to collect quantitative and qualitative data, comprising a mix of close-ended and open-ended questions. Most of the quantitative items used a five-point Likert scale. Several of the selected items are identical to items used in an annual national survey, which targets students in most of the teacher education programs in Norway.[1] These items address different aspects of the quality of teaching on campus. By including these items, it was possible to compare the mean results of the peer teaching in the present study with the mean level of faculty teaching in Norwegian teacher education. The results from the national survey are used as a benchmark to provide a tentative assessment of the relative quality of the peer teaching arrangement in the present study. Although the national student survey does not cover the PPU program, the mean results can still serve as a relevant "proxy indicator" because the data are gathered from all the other teacher education programs in Norway and provide an aggregated score that includes many students.

Some other differences between the present study and the national study need to be mentioned. First, while most items in the questionnaire were identical to those in the national survey, a few were slightly modified to better suit the teacher education context and peer teaching as the main topic. Second, while the present survey gathered data on the perceived quality of a peer teaching event that took place over two days, the national survey asks students to evaluate the whole term, including not only lessons in pedagogy but also subject-specific teaching, subject didactics, and the school-placement period.

On top of that, several unique items were included that address specific aspects of the peer teaching design and the perceived learning outcome. For example, one item asked students to compare the quality of peer teaching with faculty teaching in the first year of study. Few studies compare peer teaching with faculty-led teaching, and, to my knowledge, none have done so in the teacher education context. The students also responded to the two following open-ended questions about peer teaching as a pedagogical practice: (1) "Is there something you especially liked about the teaching activity this time?" and (2) "What do you think of the mandatory assignment 'to learn by teaching' (advantages and disadvantages)?" These questions provided valuable qualitative data because the students commented on both potential benefits and challenges related to peer teaching in teacher education.

Furthermore, the empirical analysis includes all data that were considered relevant to the three learning positions. Although many of the qualitative comments are relatively short, they still provide insight into the characteristics of these types of learning.

Peer student learning

In the first case study, as many as 81% reported satisfaction with the "overall outcome" of the peer teaching assignment. The average means score was 4.1. 16% was moderately satisfied, while only 3% were not satisfied. Regarding this issue, one student made the following comment: "I think it was good. I learned a lot this way (2)." The quantitative results show students perceived significant learning effects in all areas, not only in academic learning, but also in student motivation and improvement of teaching skills. The mean results were better than similar or identical items from a national survey from teacher education which was used as a benchmark.

Several students highlight the combination of several different types of learning. For example, on being asked what they enjoyed the most, two students stated: "It provided academic insight, and, in addition, we focused on teaching methods (1)" and "I learned a lot, both pedagogy and didactics, by following the peer teaching (1)." These statements illustrate student learning of both the subject matter and teaching methods at the same time. The students were also asked to compare the quality of the peer teaching with the faculty-led traditional lectures they had participated in during the first year of the program. Surprisingly, almost half the students (49%) stated that the quality of the peer teaching was better than a traditional lecture. Only 14% found peer teaching to be worse, and 38% assessed the quality to be approximately the same.

These results are hard to explain because all students, both high and low achievers, participated as peer teachers. It is easier to understand that experienced peer teachers at a higher educational level who are top motivated can outperform less motivated faculty teachers. But how can a whole group of inexperienced students provide high-quality teaching, and in some circumstances perhaps even the best teaching? One possible explanation can be that the other faculty-led lectures were of low, but these received relatively good student ratings.[2] In further examining the qualities of the peer student learning position, this section will distinguish between the academic learning and how engaging the lessons were.

Academic learning (the subject matter)

In general, the students perceived the academic learning quality to be of high quality. The mean score of 3.9 is also significantly higher than the national mean score of 3.5 on a similar item.[3] Nearly three out of four students (73%) were satisfied with the "subject matter in pedagogy" in the peer teaching. Twenty-two percent were moderately satisfied, while only 5% were not satisfied with the academic content.

However, a major difference in the present study and other collective peer teaching studies (Aslan, 2015, 2017) is that the students had already acquired some level of expertise in the subject matter because they were at the end of the first year of the program. The students could choose from a wide variety of topics and build on prior knowledge or interests. The students were also given a month to prepare the lesson, a substantial amount of time. In addition, they had already completed a group presentation on a pedagogical topic in the first term. Another explanation may be that the students acted as co-teachers and prepared the lessons together. It is likely that this collaboration improved the quality of the teaching.

Furthermore, two-thirds of the students had substantial practical teaching experience, already having worked at least one year in a school. One student's comment illustrates this point: "This is a really nice teaching method. I have learned a lot, both by doing it myself and observing others. When there are many skilled people in this course, this is a good way of doing it (2)." Here, the benefits of having "many skilled people" are highlighted. In comparison, faculty teachers in teacher education may have little teaching experience from school and often only teach a few days during the week.

A combination of in-depth learning and broad introductions

In the comments in the survey, several students also underlined the value of the peer student learning in different ways. One important reason was the increased relevance. One student stated, "I learned a lot by listening to peer teaching about highly relevant topics (1)." Others viewed a revisit of the same lesson content as valuable, "To get repetition on many topics (1)." In campus-based teaching in teacher education, this type of revisit is usually not prioritized except before the exam. A third student highlights the peer teaching helped summarize the first year of the teacher education: "Exciting summary of the subject matter of the first academic year (1)." The assignment challenged the peer teachers to select the most important content and transform it into an interesting lesson. Other studies have also shown significant learning effects when peer teachers must summarize a topic (Fiorella & Mayer, 2016), but there has been more uncertainty regarding the peer student learning. It indicates that the academic learning was perceived as valuable, both because it was relevant and a repetition of the lesson content.

In addition, the quantitative findings show that students have improved their critical thinking. A large majority of the students, 79%, report that they were very satisfied with their ability to reflect and think critically in their peer teaching activities. The mean score of 4.0 is high, approximately the same as the national mean score of 3.9 (The qualitative comments suggest that critical thinking is closely connected with interacting with various students' perspectives). For example, a student states, "What is most important is that we get to train our ability to think critically and think from another's perspective (2)." The comment suggests that the peer teachers contribute with other perspectives, being given the freedom to choose lesson content and teaching methods.

Moreover, the unique design in collective peer teaching supports an interesting combination of in-depth learning with a broader introduction to the subject matter in the syllabus. For example, one student commented: "Got very good insight into my own topic. Nice to get summaries from the others (2)." A second student states: "Advantages: project work, small groups, a taste of many topics, being able to go deeper into one topic (2)." On the one hand, students' participation in the various lessons ensured learning of the wider lesson content. On the other hand, students got the opportunity to examine a specific topic through their role of being a peer teacher.

More emphasis on the assessment

Furthermore, several students enjoyed that peer teaching was designed as an alternative type of formal assessment. One student emphasizes how learning was at the center of the assessment: "I have learned a lot by teaching a self-selected topic and think this is a really nice way to organize a midway exam (2)." Here, the student underlines how the assessment method centered on learning instead of control. In previous years, this assessment had been a traditional written exam. Another student highlights how the assessment method stimulated to a diverse summary of the year: "The assessment method did, in many ways, provide a varied and exciting summary of the academic content of the first year of study (1)." Positive feelings are expressed regarding how the peer teaching in its entirety created an "exciting summary" of the subject matter. While some introduced new content, others presented lesson content from previous lectures. In all lessons, the goal was to summarize the content, provide an overview, and often also to link the academic content to practical experiences. The students were satisfied with how the collective peer teaching covered most of the syllabus.

Although the peer teaching arrangement was primarily designed as a mandatory midway exam they had to pass, it was also a long-term preparation for the final exam one year later. Over two days, students provided a broad introduction of the most important topics on the syllabus. One student commented, "All the great presentations that were highly relevant for the exam (1)." In their final exam, student would need to demonstrate knowledge of the subject matter. The "midway test" was perceived as a way of initiating these preparations. From one perspective, the peer teaching arrangement was designed as a collective "teaching to the test", aiming to be as relevant to the final exam as possible.

Several students emphasized how the peer teaching was important in increasing their understanding of the subject matter. One student says, "It was a nice way to cover the syllabus (2)" and "We also covered a lot of the academic content (2)." Both these students value that the peer teaching covered a large part of the syllabus. A third student comments, "Good practice, a lot of content is reduced in a good way, summarizing (2)." The phrase "summarizing" shows that the students were part of lessons that focused on the most important topic in teacher education program.

However, since the students in the present study had not passed an exam yet, there will be some uncertainty related to quality of the content. This is why it is common to also use peer teachers who have just recently completed the exam and who are at the next educational level in the program. Because they have managed to pass the exam, this increases the authority of their teaching, and they will know better how to "teach to the test" more effectively. These peer teachers who are in their second learning cycle will be more confident in passing on their knowledge and experience. For instance, in one study in the review by Moust and Schmidt (1994), peer teachers compensate for their lack of expertise by devoting more attention to the end-of-course test.

Engaging lessons

The quantitative findings show that students perceive this teaching as more engaging. Four out of five students (81%) agreed that peer teaching allowed them to be active participants in the lessons. Only 3% of the students disagreed. The mean score of 4.3 is much higher than the national mean of 3.5. In the survey comments, one student highlights being active as the most enjoyable aspect of the learning process, "That one could be active and participating, that one could learn from each other and together (1)." A large majority of students (81%) also felt that "their peers made the teaching engaging." Only 9% disagreed. The mean score is 4.1, much higher than the national mean of 3.2, which here refers to the level of engagement in the faculty teaching. In describing this engagement, one student states, "Exciting lessons (1)", a second says, "I liked being taught by my peers very much (1)", and a third student comments, "It was very educational. It was exciting to learn from my peers (2)." All students show strong positive feelings toward the learning process. The phrase "very educational" point out significant learning gains.

On top of that, another student underlines how fun it was compared to the faculty-led lectures, "It was incredibly fun to do something else than just having lectures (1)." The notion of having fun indicates that they were able to create a more informal learning environment. Although the peer teachers were required to involve peer students actively in their lessons, it was uncertain whether the students would experience these lessons as engaging. Note that the large student group was organized into smaller classes of approximately 25 students who could be in "normal" classrooms. This made it easier to use other teaching methods compared with having lectures in the auditorium with around 80 students.

Peer teacher learning

Concerning empirical findings regarding the peer teacher learning position, this section will highlight strong student motivation, deep learning, learning through co-teaching, improvement of teaching skills, and interest in peer teaching as a teaching method.

Strong student motivation

In the survey, several students highlighted the positive learning experience when being a peer teacher. For example, one student enjoyed the most "To learn by your own teaching (1)." As many as 76% of the students were highly satisfied with their own motivation to be peer teachers ("your motivation to do this type of teaching"). Only 7% had low motivation, and 17% were moderately motivated. The mean motivational score of 4.1 stands out as significantly higher than the national mean of 3.1. It suggests that the role of being a peer teacher is a very important motivational factor in instructional design that build on learning by teaching.

Several students highlighted how they worked harder than usual because they were going to teach the topic. One student commented, "The teaching of the other students was nice, and in this way, we were "forced" to invest extra effort in one topic (2)." The emphasis on the investment of an "extra effort" indicates that students often use a substantial amount of time to acquire an understanding of the topic when preparing a lesson. It is worth noting the hard work was not experienced as optional when they were "forced" to teach. It illustrates the commitment in doing their best when being given the responsibility for a lesson. Another student emphasizes how it was necessary to build confidence about the subject matter in order to be able to teach it, "One needs to learn the content especially well to be confident enough when teaching others (…) (2)." When the students knew they were going to teach a topic, this motivated them to work harder in lesson preparations. By being responsible for others' learning in the role of a teacher, students felt that they had to understand the subject matter. The students wanted to fulfill the expected "expert role" because of their social responsibility as teachers.

Regarding potential drawbacks, several students claimed to have performance anxiety. One student commented, "I really enjoyed being a teacher for my peers, even though I was pretty nervous (1)." Here, the enjoyment and the nervousness are parts of the same process. The phrase "pretty nervous" suggests that the level of nervousness was not too high. Likewise, another student has mixed feelings, "Teaching an "unknown" class created some degree of performance anxiety, but in total, it was a beneficial learning experience (2)." Here, anxiety is linked to teaching a group of persons who one does not know.

Deep learning

Notably, some qualitative comments suggest the presence of deep learning. One student stated, "Both the assignment in itself, which offered in-depth focus, and the process in advance gave valuable contributions to my own teaching practice (2)." This student describes how the assignment provided an "in-depth focus" and the planning phase, "the process in advance" is highlighted. When taking on the role of becoming a peer teacher for the rest of the class, students are expected to become experts in their chosen subject matter area.

In addition, the description of "my own teaching practice" suggests that the student´s professional skills were developed. The students both acquired an understanding of the subject matter, but also provided practical teacher training. The emphasis in pedagogy as an academic subject will typically be less on the lesson content and more on stimulating students' reflection on different aspects of teacher's professional work.

Another student emphasizes the learning value of summarizing, "Advantages (…) training in the selection of the important content from the syllabus, training in teaching and being able to present what is most important (2)." This student underlines both learning strategies in the preparation phase through "the selection of the important content from the syllabus" and during the lesson by "being able to present what is most important." The instructional design explicitly challenged students to summarize some of the most important content from the syllabus. The peer teacher groups were given a list of relevant topics they could choose between. Because the lessons were very short, the students also had to narrow the focus on some aspects of the content in their lessons.

Learning through co-teaching

The peer teaching in the present study was conducted as co-teaching in small groups. As many as 79% of the students were satisfied with how the peer teaching developed their collaborative skills. Only 7% were not satisfied, and 14% were moderately satisfied. Two or three peer teachers worked together to prepare a lesson for the rest of the group. The co-teachers had to read about the topic and discuss the academic content with each other. In general, this type of collaboration increases the likelihood of producing high-quality peer teaching because the co-teachers can support each other in their preparations (Duran, 2017).

Several students remarked that they enjoyed the collaboration in the small peer teacher groups. One student stated, "It's very useful with group work, and to make a lesson is very good practice (2)." This student also emphasizes how the assignment provided relevant teacher training, highlighting that peer teachers not only learn about the subject matter in this process. Another student describes how co-teaching improves the students' collaborative skills. On top of that, one student underscores how close co-teaching strengthened peer relations, "One gets better acquainted through collaborative planning (2)." In co-teaching, students help each other in optimizing the lesson, and during this process they also develop several other skills.

A potential drawback is that some students do less work. However, none of the students complained about this. Still, a few students were not satisfied with the co-teaching. One student commented: "Disadvantage: It is always more work when being in groups because one must plan and coordinate, and one often prepares a bit different. I prefer to work more independently. Advantage: It was instructive (2)." Lesson preparations in co-teaching can be more time-consuming and conflict can emerge when students want to do the lesson in different ways.

Improving teaching skills

The survey results show that a majority of students (57%) felt that the peer teaching developed their vocational and subject-specific skills. Thirty-six percent mentioned this happened to some degree and 7% to a small degree. The mean score of 3.8 is 0.3 points above the national mean score on the same item. Some students also highlight the value of being able to practice their teaching skills. A student comments, "It´s nice to get self-training in classroom management." Classroom management is a core skill in teacher education. Several students describe how their teaching competence was enhanced through the combination of teaching and observing other students' teaching. One student says, "Very good arrangement, instructive both to stand and teach and be a student (2)."

Notably, some students highlighted the importance of integrating the peer teaching into the assessment system. For example, one student stated, "I really liked that the mid-term exam required us to teach (1)." This student expresses positive feelings related to how teaching became a part of the exam. This was perhaps easier because this was not a "high-stakes" exam. The peer teaching performances were not graded, and the threshold for passing was not very high; it primarily required that the students taught the lesson. Still, other student comments show that several students express a significant degree of performance anxiety, with the formal assessment raising the stakes.

Interest in peer teaching as a teaching method

Many of these students even wanted to use this teaching method in their own school classes in the future. 82% answered that they intend to use peer teaching as a teaching method in school. As many as 60% "agree completely," which indicate a strong belief in the learning potential of this teaching method. Only 7% find it not to be relevant. Eighty-one percent also find collective peer teaching to be a method that is an effective way of learning. Only 5% disagree. These results are surprisingly positive as this pedagogical practice appears not to be widespread in Norwegian schools. They mark an attitudinal change and the emergence of new ways of thinking about learning and teaching.

Furthermore, three out of four students (77%) reported satisfaction with how peer teaching influenced their ability to "think in new ways," while only 17% were moderately satisfied. Here, the mean score of 4.0 is much higher than the national average of 3.5, showing that it is possible to experiment with new teaching methods at campus which later can be used in schools. A student highlighted the innovative aspect of this pedagogical practice, "Great. It was enlightening. Cool thing that you tried doing something new (2)." These findings indicate that peer teaching can lead to attitudinal change.

Collective peer learning

This section presents empirical findings related to collective peer learning, highlighting five different areas related to whole-group learning.

Increasing lesson diversity

First, the peer teaching arrangement was organized as a multitude of short lessons, which requires all students to rotate on being peer teachers. Several students highlight how this created variation in a positive way. One student says, "Appreciate observing and listening to other students presenting varied topics (…) (1)." Another student mentions the "many interesting theoretical topics (…) (1)." On the one hand, the variation spurred an interest in the subject matter and the academic learning.

Others underlined the value of observing a wide variety of teaching methods. One student said, "I enjoyed teaching and also getting ideas from others who were teaching (1)." Another student commented, "I picked up many useful 'tricks' (1)." A third student stated, "It was very interesting to observe different methods and techniques others used in their teaching and useful to be teaching each other (1)." Several students emphasized how they could learn by observing different teaching methods being used, which could potentially enhance their teaching repertoire.

However, an important difference in collective peer teaching is that students learn both by being peer teachers and by observing other peer teachers. A fourth student underscores how it was inspiring to observe others, "I learned a lot and also got inspiration from the other students on how I can organize my teaching (1)." This student appears to have also gotten ideas on how to improve their own teaching in the school. The variety of peer lessons provided rich opportunities to compare how peer teachers addressed the same challenge.

Furthermore, one student claims that the variation in teaching methods made it easier to participate in the lessons, "The best thing was the different teaching methods. It is easier to pay attention if there is variation in the presentations, which there was a lot of (1)." In the faculty-led lectures it would typically be more focused on the subject matter, less on the teaching methods.

The large degree of variation was made possible because each lesson only lasted 25 minutes. Fourteen different topics were covered during two days of teaching in two separate tracks. Each peer teacher groups could choose their own teaching method, resulting in exposure to a multitude of teaching methods because of the many short lessons.

Several students also highlight the time-efficiency of this type of teaching: One student commented, "To be introduced to so much great and varied teaching in such a short time (1)." Another student also points out the time-efficiency of this peer teaching, "What is positive, is that we have covered many topics in a short time (2)." The organization of the peer teaching made it possible to cover a broad scope of topics in the different sessions. This peer teaching design is very different from how a faculty teacher was usually responsible for a complete day of teaching, covering just one topic. In ordinary school-placement periods, students would not necessarily either get the opportunity to observe equally many different lessons.

Furthermore, some students even highlighted the learning value of both being able to learn about the subject matter and teaching methods at the same time. One student stated, "Variation concerning both topics and teaching methods (1)", another commented, "To observe how other peers teach, get inspired, and at the same time go through many different relevant topics (1)." In addition, a student emphasizes how the learning value is related to all the different student background, "It was educational and enriching to be taught by such a diversity of students with different educational background, work experience, age range and nationality! (1)." Here, the student links diversity to differences in background that manifests itself through different types of teaching in the classroom. The personal teaching styles became present when students were allowed to use their unique teaching competence, like one peer teacher group who used musical instruments.

The benefits of variation increased when it involved all aspects of the peer teaching. One student even underlines the value of observing differences in the quality of the peer teaching, "It was useful to see other students teach, both to get inspiration and to see what we do but be conscious about avoiding (2)." The phrase "conscious about avoiding" indicates that reflection around the teaching practice is more important than observing best practices. There is value in comparing lessons of different quality. The development of proficient teaching skills may not only be about adapting to best practice, but to better understand how to avoid certain teaching behaviors. Good teaching is not necessarily about observing one correct way of teaching.

A community of equals

Several students underline the value of being part of a community of learners. For example, one student comments, "I liked that it was based on our lessons (1)." It was motivating to manage their own learning processes. Another student highlights how the student group learned of each other, "Learned a lot by observing each other in action (1)." The phrase "in action" shows that the students also learn by observing each other. A third student emphasizes how the students were able to motivate each other, "Nice to observe the other students in 'practice'. It makes you sharpen up. Great that there were a lot of activities (2)." When students observed others' engagement, this motivated them to make good lessons. Likewise, a student states, "To learn by observing each other's teaching, and we inspired each other (2)." The peer observation inspired the students.

Furthermore, another student highlights the strong degree of group equality. One student states, "We learned of "equals" and got to know each other better in the group (2)." The phrase "equals" points toward a strong feeling of learning together and being in a symmetrical relationship. When all students make important contributions, this strengthens the feeling of a shared responsibility for the learning process. This is possible when all students specialize in one specific area, making it easier to contribute with valuable knowledge to the rest of the class. When everyone contributes, the mutual interdependence in the large group increases and helps strengthen the connections between the students. The learning relationship is also more symmetrical compared with when student teachers observe their practicum teacher, who is typically considered to be an expert teacher. It is also different from including "cross-level" peer teachers at a higher educational level.

Learning by switching roles

Notably, several students describe how they enjoyed being in different learning positions, switching between being in a peer learner and a peer teacher. One student says, "I think it was incredibly enlightening to be both a teacher and a student (2)." The phrase "incredibly enlightening" indicates significant learning in being allowed to switch rapidly between being a peer student and a peer teacher. For two days, students would be responsible for one lesson and observe around 10 other lessons. This made it possible to compare their own peer teaching with how other students solved the same task with a short time span. Similarly, another student says, "I liked how peer teaching was organized between the students. We learned a lot by listening to the others and by making our own lesson! (1)." On the one hand, this student highlights the value of the complete organization of the peer teaching arrangement. On the other, the student describes a powerful learning process that emerges in the interplay between self-observation and attentive observation of others.

However, a disadvantage is that performance anxiety appears to have had a negative effect on some students' learning. One student stated: "I really liked this way of doing it. I was afraid that I would be so anxious that I wouldn't be able to pay attention to the other's lessons, but it went very well

(2)." This student appears to have managed to cope with the anxiety level, while others felt this had a negative influence on their learning experience. For example, one student commented: "I was a bit nervous so I wasn't able to pay attention to everything the others said (2)." This student focused so much on own teaching that it was a distraction when participating in the other lessons. For this student, the performance anxiety may have had a negative influence on the learning experience. Likewise, another student stated, "However, the focus is very much on your own work and less on others (2)." The disadvantage with allowing everyone to participate in the same arrangement in just a few days is that some students appear to have become too fixated on their own lesson. A third student underlines that this was more of a problem just before they are going to do their teaching session, "Very good, the disadvantage is that you get distracted before your own presentation (2)." The intensity of the distraction was particularly a problem immediately before their own presentation.

Although performance anxiety is normal and an important part of the motivation when preparing for a test or an exam, the level of anxiety may become too high. Students remarked that they learned a lot about their own topic in their role as peer teachers, but the instructional design may have reduced their motivation to fully pay attention to others teaching. The risk is that there is less learning about other topics in the curriculum, and less coverage of the breadth of topics.

Scaling up the peer feedback

The peer students were allowed to evaluate each lesson immediately afterward. This would usually include a few brief comments (approximately five minutes) and the opportunity to write anonymous written feedback in an online questionnaire. The rubric "two stars and a wish" was used to encourage praise, but also constructive critique. The empirical findings show that 65% of the students were highly satisfied with the peer feedback. Twenty-one percent were moderately satisfied, and only 14% were not satisfied. The mean score on this item is 3.7, significantly higher than the national mean of 3.4. This result is surprisingly positive since the oral feedback after the lesson was brief, only allowing for a few comments. In addition, several students chose not to give any written feedback to the peer teachers after the lesson.

In the survey, several students also commented on the value of receiving peer feedback. One student says, "To teach and present, and get a nice response (1)." This student highlights the value of the praise. Another student says, "Very nice to be a part of others' teaching and get a lot of advice relevant to your own teaching. Also, nice to have a presentation (2)." The phrase "get a lot of advice" suggests that there was value in increasing the amount of the feedback. A third student even highlighted the learning value of giving feedback, "A good way to learn, I think it was useful to observe others presenting, especially when the task is to give feedback (2)." Here, the students suggest that it is more valuable to observe others if the task is to give feedback afterward. When everyone is required to give feedback, this can sharpen their focus and attention during the lesson.

Developing knowledge collectively

As previously mentioned, the midway exam also allowed the students to share their knowledge with each other in different ways. Each peer teacher group was assigned to summarize a topic, both through a lesson and by writing a summary. The complete collection of student contribution gave a more comprehensive overview of the various topics in the syllabus. For instance, one student states, "A nice way to get a better overview of parts of the syllabus and create more engagement on different topics (1)." The goal with the summaries was to avoid fragmentation and give everybody a role in a collective effort to produce common knowledge in the class. Together the whole group were able to produce an overview of most of the academic content in the syllabus. One student thinks the peer teaching made it possible to cover the syllabus in a smart way, "I think it worked well and was a nice way of acquiring a lot of the syllabus 'for free' (1)." The phrase "for free" indicates a perception of being part of a collective effort in covering all the relevant content in the course. The written summaries provided a transparent overview of the complete peer teaching arrangement in both parallel sessions.

When the students became their own teachers, they also became collectively responsible for producing content relevant to preparing for the exam. From one perspective, the peer teaching arrangement turned the notion of "teaching to the test" upside down because the students, not the teacher, did this work.

Although same-level peer teachers can provide peer students with advice on what knowledge is important, there is still a significant level of uncertainty regarding the academic content. Most students will want the teaching to be relevant for the assessment, but they cannot teach with the same level of certainty as cross-level peer teachers who have passed the course. These peer teachers will usually explain and connect the different important concepts and topics in the course with more confidence (Lockspeiser et al., 2008). On the other hand, there is less risk that same-level peer teachers will have lessons that are too instrumental or focused on the exam because they have not yet completed it. Another difference is that there will not just be one peer teacher, but many different peer teachers who provide independent summaries of different topics. However, the disadvantage was the lack of attempts to synthesize the topics.

Notes

1 The national survey (Studiebarometeret) includes only teacher education programs at a bachelor and master level that last a minimum of three terms. This is why the one-year teacher education program has been excluded from the survey. The annual survey is conducted in the second and fifth year of a wide range of educational programs. In the present study, the national results from fall 2018 are used. At this time, the national survey was sent to 65,000 students in 1,800 study programs, including teacher education programs, such as Primary and Lower Secondary Teacher Education for Years 1–7, Primary and Lower Secondary Teacher Education for Years 5–10, and master's degree programs in teacher education (five years) with specialization in different subject areas.
2 In the first-year student evaluation of the teacher education program, 59% of the students were satisfied, 33% moderately satisfied, and 8% not satisfied.
3 This item refers to the perceived satisfaction with the faculty teaching of theoretical subject matter in teacher education.

4 Second case study—collective peer teaching in teacher education

The collective peer teaching design

In the second case study, student teachers were assigned to take over the responsibility for most of the lessons and rotate on being peer teachers. Here, the educational context is one of the largest teacher education institutions in Norway. During autumn 2022, the collective peer teaching design was implemented in a mandatory 15 credit course in pedagogy, the fifth and final year of the Primary and Lower Secondary Teacher Education for Years 1–7. Most of the student teachers are in their mid-twenties.

A total of 155 students followed the course which was offered autumn 2022. Class size ranged from 35 to 45 students. The lessons are typically organized as a two-hour lecture by the faculty staff early in the week. Later in the week, the large group is split into four smaller classes who have separate two-hour lessons on the same topic. To allow all students to be peer teachers, seven of the 11 lessons in the course were organized in this way. There were three students in most of the peer teacher teams, but there were also some with two and four. Compared with the first case study, an important difference is how the peer teaching comprised most of the lessons in the whole course.

In implementing peer teaching, several major changes were done in the organization of the lessons. To provide guidance to the students before the peer teaching, the traditional lecture early in the week was reorganized as a pre-mentoring session for the four peer teacher groups who were going to teach the following week. These sessions would usually start with a short lecture on the topic and the students would get the rest of the time to plan a lesson and share their ideas with the other peer teacher groups.

The disadvantage was that the rest of the students did not get any teaching, reducing the total amount of teaching in the course. This was done with no extra resources related to the new instructional design. However, because students complained about the lack of lectures, the last three last pre-mentoring sessions were both videorecorded and broadcasted live on the internet.

The students were typically responsible for one lesson that lasted around thirty minutes. Every week in each class, the student teams would either be responsible for two separate lessons or collaborate in planning a two-hour lesson. Since peer teaching was the dominant pedagogical practice, the peer teacher teams were assigned to various tasks outside of the classroom. One week, they were responsible for a tour in the local school museum, another week they designed a city tour for the students with a geo app. One of the lessons at campus was also quite different because the teams had to arrange a workshop on digital storytelling.

In the previous years, the students could choose freely if they wanted to attend the lessons in the course. They were only required to pass an exam at the end of the semester and complete a few simple assignments during the semester. Consequently, only around 30% of the students attended the face-to-face lessons in smaller classes autumn 2021. Because of the low turn-out, students had to participate in a minimum of 60% of the lessons. This would ensure that a relatively large group, from 25 to 35 students, would participate every week.

After the lesson, all students were assigned to give the peer teachers feedback. The peer teacher group also had to write a reflection text afterward based on the feedback (1,000–2,000 words). In addition, students were required to write an individual reflection about peer teaching as one of five mandatory topics in the term paper. The collective peer teaching was considered relevant for several of the learning objectives in the course, especially the capacity to innovate pedagogical practices and participate in professional learning communities.

The research study

In the second case study, an online survey was employed to explore student teachers' perceptions of their participation in peer teaching. All students enrolled in the course were encouraged to complete this survey during the final class session. This survey served a dual purpose: it provided a course evaluation for the students and also supplied data for this research study. Out of 155 students enrolled in the course, 92 participated in the survey, yielding a response rate of 59%. It is important to note that while a majority of present students completed the survey, a considerable portion of non-respondents existed, indicating a potential for non-response bias.

The survey instrument was designed to gather both quantitative and qualitative data, incorporating a combination of closed-ended and open-ended questions. The majority of the quantitative items utilized a five-point Likert scale, with items focusing on various facets of peer teaching quality and the students' perceived learning outcomes. The open-ended questions were specifically tailored to address various aspects of peer teaching as a pedagogical practice. These questions provided insightful qualitative data as students provided commentary on both the potential advantages and challenges associated with this teaching approach.

The survey data provide insight into the subjective learning experiences of the students and their perceptions of the efficacy of peer teaching. The empirical analysis includes data that are relevant to the three learning positions. Although some of the qualitative comments are relatively short, they still provide valuable information about these different types of learning.

In addition, the researcher conducted observations during half of the peer lessons. These observational data served to complement and contextualize the findings derived from the survey responses. This combined approach provided a more comprehensive picture of the students' experiences and perceptions related to peer teaching within the course.

Peer student learning

In the second case study, the mean overall score was 3.1 for the perceived learning outcomes of collective peer teaching. Only 34% of the students report of a high overall learning outcome. Forty-four percent state a moderate learning outcome, while 22% claim they had a low level of learning. Compared with the first case study, the mean score is significantly lower. Being asked whether peer teaching is better than traditional seminars with a teacher educator, the students are split. Thirty-two percent claim peer teaching is better, 32% of the same level, and 36% state peer teaching is of a lower level.

How do we explain these differences in perceived learning outcomes, both within the student group and between the two collective peer teaching designs? Regarding the peer student learning position, the findings cover the following four areas: professionally relevant learning, academic learning, active learning, and relevance for the summative assessment.

Professionally relevant learning

Most students find collective peer teaching to be relevant for their work as professional teachers. Thirty-five percent experienced the participation as highly relevant for their future work as a teacher, while 36% stated that it was moderately relevant. In addition, 28% found it to be less relevant. Several students claim this type of learning activity is relevant because it resembles professional practice, also leading to a stronger motivation. The disadvantage was that students had too much freedom in deciding whether they wanted to include content in the lesson from the syllabus.

The empirical findings show that many as 69% (mean 3.7) of the students agree that peer teaching have addressed core questions in the teaching profession. Regarding this issue, one student states:

> I feel I learn more about myself as a teacher and different factors that are important to have in mind when I have completed my education. But I

feel that I have not learned that much theoretical knowledge until the last weeks, perhaps more practical knowledge throughout the semester.

This student highlights the opportunity to reflect on the professional role as a teacher. It indicates that peer student learning is orientated toward practical knowledge acquisition, less toward theoretical knowledge in the lessons.

Academic learning

Regarding academic learning, the students are divided in their perceptions of the academic learning of peer teaching. Thirty-six percent agree that they have elaborated on the subject matter and the syllabus, 34% mention that this has happened only to some degree, while 31% report a low level of academic learning. Several students report experiencing substantial variation in the quality of the different peer lessons.

Students provide several explanations concerning the lack of academic learning. Some suggest that it should have been mandatory to present content from the syllabus in the peer lessons. Many peer teachers did not attempt to integrate the theoretical knowledge with the learning activities or practical experiences in the lesson. They struggled to connect the fun learning parts with the academic learning. For example, one student tells this made the teaching less serious. The lesson objective should also have been clarified. Besides this, some students think the 30-minute lessons were too short. One student claims it was a lot of activity and reflection, but less in-depth learning because of the lack of time.

Equally significant, some students were critical because one could not know whether the lesson was trustworthy. For example, one student underlines state that the lecturers are the persons who really know what they are talking about. Others experienced that the lesson content did not offer any new perspectives. One student claims that most peer teachers only reproduced knowledge from previous semesters, leading to little new learning.

Additionally, because there were few lectures in the course, this reinforced the lack of academic learning. For instance, one states:

> I think the learning outcome both of being a peer teacher and learning from other students have been limited this semester. I do not feel that we have gotten the overview and the context we need, with the help of teachers who have a broader perspective and more academic knowledge than us. Instead, the result has been to reproduce the syllabus or opinionate based on what one has experienced. I wish we had more lessons with the teachers.

Several students claim that many of the peer teachers reproduced subject matter knowledge which they had already learned in previous years. This limited the learning value. Because the formal teachers had little time to comment on the subject matter, students felt there was little deep learning.

Active learning

Notably, a majority of 61% (mean 3.7) of the students agree that they were engaged in the lessons. Only 9% were not engaged, while 30% reported a moderate level of engagement. Several students commented on their motivation, and some even mentioned that they were more active than normal:

> During some periods, studying will not be the main priority. Then this (read: collective peer teaching) is a way of forcing us to take more responsibility for each other as students. Although one could say that some of the work just covers what is necessary, one still pays extra attention.

This student has attended more lessons. Others emphasize feelings of joy, "It was surprisingly good. I did not think that the peer teaching lessons would be that fun." Regarding the lack of engagement, one student claimed this was because the academic learning was not challenging enough.

Relevance for the summative assessment

Another aspect with peer student learning is its relevance for the summative assessment. The empirical findings show that students are divided in how relevant the peer teaching was for the semester paper in this course. Forty-one percent think the peer teaching was highly relevant, 30% only moderately relevant, and as many as 29% claim it was of little relevance for the semester paper. These findings suggest that students did not perceive the learning process to be completely aligned with the exam. For example, one potential drawback can be illustrated by one student who stated that the main emphasis was on their own lesson topic, but less on other topics in the syllabus. Likewise, other research studies have found that student motivation is closely connected to how the learning activities are relevant for the exam or the final summative assessment (Harlen et al., 2002).

Peer teacher learning

Regarding peer teacher learning, the students were asked about the perceived learning value of being peer teachers. This included the post-lesson work that required the peer teacher group to write a reflection text. On this item, 50% report a high learning outcome. Thirty percent had a moderate level, while 19% claimed that they had a low level of learning (mean score 3.4).

60 *Second case study—collective peer teaching in teacher education*

In the subsequent section, we will delve deeper into the considerable disparities observed in the outcomes. There may be several different explanations. First, the co-teaching does not appear to have had a negative influence on the peer teacher learning. Eighty-nine percent report that the collaboration with the peer teachers was very good. It shows that co-teaching was a success, even though the students could not choose their collaborative partners. Still, one student claims the group dynamics had a negative effect because group minimized their preparation effort because a few persons in the group were not motivated.

Second, there are mixed opinions present in how the peer teachers experience the academic learning. In the peer teacher role, 36% state a significant degree of academic learning, 37% report moderate learning, and as many as 27% claim they had a low level of academic learning. A key reason is that during the city tour and digital storytelling workshop, which occurred in two of the weekly sessions, peer teachers had minimal involvement in teaching. Some students mentioned not gaining any exposure to peer teaching, making it difficult for them to respond to questions related to the subject. A second explanation is that some students state they did little work in preparing the lesson, therefore, they learned less about the subject matter. Students were only given one week to prepare the lesson, which the opportunity to learn in the preparation period. For example, one student tells it became more "important to get the task done instead of optimizing the performance." This statement shows the presence of indicates minimum strategies.

Notably, a majority of 54% of peer teachers stated it was very enjoyable to choose their own teaching methods. Thirty-two percent were somewhat enjoyable, while 15% had little fun (mean score 3.4). This freedom of choice appears to have had a positive influence on motivation. Still, the overall peer teacher motivation to do peer teaching is mixed. Thirty-three percent had a strong motivation, 28% a moderate motivation, while as many as 40% were not motivated. Compared with the first case study, the peer teacher motivation is much lower. Although some students report being motivated by the social responsibility for their peers, several other factors have a negative influence. One important explanation is the lack of interest in the subject matter. Twenty-nine percent were not interested in the topic they were assigned to teach. Almost half (44%) were moderately interested, and only 28% were really interested in the subject matter. Not letting students choose the lesson topic had a negative influence on the motivation.

A second explanation is increased stress. Twenty percent report having a high level of performance anxiety and 23% claim it was not enjoyable to lead the whole-class discussions. Observations showed that many peer teachers avoided discussing topics, and they also asked few questions to the whole student group. Twenty-four percent felt it was "much more" stressful to stand in front of peers compared with children in school. For example, one student comments:

Table 4.1 Correlation between peer teacher motivation and various aspects of the peer teacher role

Items	Correlation coefficient (Spearman's rho)	p-value (N)
Fun to choose teaching methods	0.60	<0.001** (91)
Lesson content was interesting	0.59	<0.001** (90)
Fun to lead whole-class discussions	0.42	<0.001** (89)
Performance anxiety	0.36	<0.001** (91)
Quality of the collaboration with other peer teachers	−0.26	0.013* (89)

*: $p < 0.05$, **: $p < 0.01$

> I think the peer teacher role has been more stressing compared with teaching students [in school], because I feel responsible for the [peer] students' learning in a topic I actually need to learn myself. Do not feel I am the right person to teach, and I am worried that the students will no learn as much about the topic from me compared with a lecturer.

This comment reveals that the performance anxiety is at least partly related to students' lack of background knowledge about the topic. Because there were few faculty-led lectures in the course, this increased the pressure on producing high-quality peer lessons. Conversely, one might expect that the students would have been better able to tackle this situation because they are expected to participate in professional learning communities with colleagues in school. Table 4.1 provides an overview of how peer teacher motivation correlated with other items in the survey.

Importantly, we see that the interest in the lesson content is strongly correlated with peer teacher motivation. It indicates that collective peer teaching design was not optimized in this case study because students were not allowed to freely choose a lesson topic of their own interest.

Furthermore, despite many stating a low level of peer teacher learning and motivation, almost half of the students still report (45%) feeling a strong sense of accomplishment after the lesson. Thirty-nine percent felt it some degree, while only 17% did not report of any sense of mastery. This suggests that despite experiencing negative emotions throughout their educational journey, some students may have still managed to boost their self-confidence. In this context, the process of learning as a peer teacher can potentially be likened to a "learning pit" (Nottingham, 2015). In being asked how important it is to let students do peer teaching in teacher education, only 24% do not think it is important. As many as 35% find it to be really important, 34% of moderate importance. It indicates that most students appreciate the learning potential in this type of assignment.

Collective peer learning

This section shows empirical findings that is orientated toward collective peer learning, highlighting six different areas.

Professional learning community

First, most students experience being part of a professional learning community through the peer teaching. Sixty-six percent students agree and only 8% disagree. For example, one student highlights the combination of reflection and knowledge sharing, "The emphasis is not on cramming the syllabus, but on autonomous reflection and use of knowledge, sharing in a community instead of competition." Students describe a learning environment dominated by responsibility for their own learning. Another student claims the main difference from ordinary lessons was the increase in autonomy, although a third student mentions that it was a bit too much freedom. However, many students appear to have been less interested in reusing the shared digital resources, indicating that the other resources in the course were sufficient.

The organization of the lessons

Second, several students stated that there should have been more time to reflect and discuss the topics, to strengthen the in-depth learning. Instead, the students learned a little bit about several different topics. Many of the students would have preferred more lesson time when they were peer teachers. To strengthen the time for deep learning, students even suggest that some of the other mandatory assignments in the course should be removed. In this final year of the program, the students are also busy beginning to prepare their work with the master thesis, while many already work part-time in schools.

The benefits of observational learning

A third important finding is that half of the students report significant observational learning. Forty-two percent (mean 3.1) claim they learned by observing how fellow students teach, and 53% (mean 3.4) learned by observing the diversity of different teaching methods. Forty-eight percent (mean 3.3) even report that they learned by observing and comparing variations in the quality of the peer teaching. It illustrates there can be learning value also in observing lesson of poor quality. In addition, several students comment on the benefits of observational learning. For example, one student says: "(…) Advantages: Good class environment, many good and interesting discussions, interesting to watch others' teaching. (…)." However, one should note that approximately one of four students report little observational learning, while one of four are neutral in this issue. Besides this, other students describe how the peer lessons created more variation. For example, one student states: "(…) It becomes easier to pay attention since it is varied, and we students get to participate a lot (…)." This comment highlights the benefits of increasing the number of lessons and teachers.

Collective peer feedback

Regarding the peer feedback, only 15% report a high level of learning from in the peer teaching. Thirty-two percent report moderate learning, while as many of half of the students (53%) experienced little learning. How do we explain the perceived low level of learning?

First, the peer teachers were encouraged to make their own evaluative questions, but most ended up using the "two stars and a wish"-rubric. In the comments, many students state they only received short comments, praise in vague terms, little constructive critique, and few comments on how to improve the teaching. There were substantial disparities in the quality of the peer feedback. For example, one student claims there was significant learning in the peer feedback because it was specific in what was good and could be done differently. Other comments point to a feedback culture is dominated by "minimum strategies," with the result that gave recommendations on how to improve the peer teaching. In contrast, most of the students were satisfied with the teacher feedback from the formal teacher which typically addressed specific "didactical challenges."

Importantly, one student suggests that the whole student group need to learn how to give more relevant peer feedback. The students are divided on whether the oral feedback should be given in front of the whole class or not. One-third want the feedback to be shared in the class (38%), one-third want it private (32%), while one-third are undecided (31%). For example, one student claimed that a public peer feedback in the whole class reduced the lesson time, which was unfortunate. It would have been enough just to write comments in the online form. Honest public feedback also requires that the students trust each other.

Class atmosphere

A large majority of the students (74%) think the class atmosphere has been very good and the quality of the relationship between the students to be very good (70%). For example, one student claims collective peer teaching leads to a much better class atmosphere because it is fun to attend the seminars. Another student claims a traditional teacher-directed lessons would have resulted in lower attendance and a worse class atmosphere. A third student also states that the very good class atmosphere led to good and learning-rich discussions.

Note that 22% felt the quality of the group relationship between the students was medium, while only 8% did not think the quality of the relationship was good. Likewise, 20% thought the atmosphere was acceptable, while only 6% found it to be poor. This was especially present in one of the four classes (seminar groups) in the course. These students report lower perceived learning on the quality of the peer feedback, lack of engagement, and less academic learning.[1] These results are a bit surprising since the students only meet each other two hours a week. Over the semester, it appears that different class cultures evolved. Perhaps the peer teaching made the stakes higher and the emotions more tense.

Fair learning

Notably, a relatively large group found the peer teaching to be unfair. As many as 37% of the students claimed the division of the workload in the class was unfair, 20% were uncertain, and 43% felt it was fair. Although students diverge in their opinions, many comment on the peer lessons being too different from each other. The museum visit required more planning, while the city tour and the workshop in digital storytelling demanded less work. One student felt that it required more time to prepare the theoretically orientated lessons.

Besides this, several other factors increased the unfairness. One student did not get to say anything during the lesson. Another student found it more stressful to have the peer teaching lesson, close to the deadline for the semester paper. This gave less time to write the paper than others. A third student claimed others got to teach the fun topics. On top of that, one student is concerned about the quality of the teaching when it is completely dependent on the peers:

> The biggest difference has been my own concern with the academic content this semester, which has been almost completely dependent on my peers. This has made me very worried since we are very different students with very different effort and expectations of mastery.

Even though all four classes taught the same course, the peer teacher opted to present the material in a variety of ways. The absence of a uniform teaching approach was seen as stressful by some, as they believed it could potentially result in an inequitable foundation for the final assessment.

Note

1 See the Appendix, *Table 9.16* Perceived learning outcome of peer teaching split on the four different seminar groups.

5 Perspectives on peer teacher learning

Peer teacher learning is one of the three major learning positions in collective peer teaching. The empirical findings show that this type of learning has four important characteristics. *First*, it is often associated with stronger motivation than usual because of the social responsibility for others learning. It involves both positive feelings of joy and pride, and potentially negative feelings like stress and performance anxiety. *Second,* peer teaching learning requires the use of higher-order teaching skills. It involves both organizing strategies and metacognitive skills in planning and evaluating the lesson. During the lesson, elaborate strategies can be used to ask reflective questions and think aloud by explaining the subject matter to others. *Third*, this learning position builds on an iterative learning process that moves through three phases, the lesson preparation phase, the lesson enactment phase, and the lesson evaluation phase. *Fourth*, peer teacher learning is not only directed toward the subject matter but also includes the development of professional skills such as teaching proficiency.

Higher-order thinking skills

Background

According to Fiorella and Mayer (2016), learning by teaching is well-studied and well-supported in having consistently shown to improve student learning. It involves a combination of advanced learning strategies that together supports generative learning. It lets the individual makes sense of information by mentally reorganizing and integrating it with one's existing knowledge. It involves selecting the most relevant information to include in one's explanation, organizing the material into a coherent structure that can be understood by others, and elaborating on the material. During the act of teaching, the individual applies the knowledge to a new situation. It can also include a combination of several other generative learning strategies, such as self-explaining, summarizing, drawing, and enacting. Here, transfer is more important than rote learning outcomes such as recall (Fiorella & Mayer, 2016).

In peer teacher learning, simple memorization is not enough because the peer teacher will need to understand the subject matter to teach it. In preparing a lesson, the peer teacher must analyze, synthesize, evaluate, and create new knowledge. In this section, four of the most prominent strategies will be discussed: Learning by asking reflective questions, learning by explaining, learning by summarizing, and learning metacognitive skills.

Learning by asking reflective questions (during the lesson)

First, the quality of the peer interaction is considered an important part of the peer teacher learning process. However, there is a risk that the peer teachers merely restate the material with minimal elaboration, limiting themselves to simple knowledge telling (Duran, 2017; Fiorella & Mayer, 2016; Topping et al., 2017). High-quality interaction will often stimulate peer teachers to discuss different issues with the students. One example is if peer students ask the peer teacher to further explain the material and elaborate on the topic. The peer teacher will usually feel socially obliged to provide a relevant response which can potentially trigger deeper generative learning. If the peer teacher is not able to provide a good answer, it can trigger a motivation to acquire more knowledge about the topic to improve the quality of the explanation (Fiorella & Mayer, 2016). Being involved in asking and answering questions is considered to be more valuable for learning than just presenting a topic (Kobayashi, 2019; Roscoe, 2014; Roscoe & Chi, 2008).

Especially in the second case study, peer students seldom asked reflective questions to the peer teacher in the whole-class discussions. There was little discussion that addressed misconceptions or requests for clarifications. The peer teachers also asked few reflective questions to the whole student group. When peer students made any comments, the peer teachers seldom asked follow-up questions. Although the formal teacher encouraged the peer teachers to do more of this type of interaction, it remained a small. One explanation is the lack of time because the lessons were very short. Another explanation is that peer teachers wanted to avoid plenary discussions because this could potentially put them in an uncomfortable situation not knowing the answer to a question. A third explanation is that the peer teachers were not aware of the discrepancy between their espoused theories and their theories-in-use (Argyris & Schon, 1992). IRE communication dominated (Cazden, 2001). These findings suggest that teacher educators need to provide better guidance to peer teachers in how to avoid knowledge-telling practices. Since the peer teacher is not an expert on the content, critical scrutiny of the explanations and dialogue becomes even more important (Duran & Topping, 2017; Kobayashi, 2019; Roscoe, 2014; Roscoe & Chi, 2008; Topping et al., 2017).

Learning by explaining

Second, peer teacher learning occurs when presenting or explaining the lesson content to others. Research by Fiorella and Mayer (2013) shows that students who taught the material performed better than those who completed a comprehension test. Learning is enhanced when individuals verbalize their own thoughts for the purpose of helping another person compared with just demonstrating self-mastery on a test. Studies have also shown that actual peer teaching has a more positive effect on learning than just expecting to teach somebody, but not actually doing it. Explaining the learning material to others allows rehearsing and reviewing the material, which consolidates and reinforces the knowledge one already possesses. It can support the construction of a deeper understanding of the subject matter (Fiorella & Kuhlmann, 2020; Fiorella & Mayer, 2016).

In both case studies, students also presented and explained a topic. They did not just engage the students in active learning. However, the presentation periods were often quite short, especially in the second case study. Nor was there always a clear link between the selected lesson topics and the semester paper. This may have decreased the motivation to provide a high-quality explanation when it was not perceived as directly relevant for the final summative assessment.

Furthermore, the quality of the learning will depend on how the explanations are given. There will be less learning if one simply restates the content from the syllabus. Instead, one should use elaborative learning strategies to reorganize and integrate the material with existing knowledge (Fiorella & Mayer, 2016; Roscoe, 2014; Roscoe & Chi, 2008). Especially in the second case study, some students chose to read aloud their presentation from a manuscript which limited the benefits of the peer teacher learning process. Others used "think aloud" strategies and were able to integrate the academic content with their personal experiences.

Explanations can also be supported by drawing something on the blackboard or by using computer tools, to depict the content of a lesson (Fiorella & Mayer, 2016). In the case studies, the peer teachers seldom use the blackboard during the lesson. Most peer teachers preferred using a power point, which limited the benefits of this type of learning strategy. Note that the process of learning by explaining may begin already in the preparation phase. Peer teachers might rehearse what they are going to say in the forthcoming lesson. The learning effects of self-explaining are well documented (Fiorella & Mayer, 2016). In addition, the peer teacher team might use time explaining different academic issues to each other.

Learning by summarizing

Effective summarizing challenges peer teachers to concisely state the main ideas in their own words. It is different from copying words or phrases verbatim from a book (Fiorella & Mayer, 2016). Other studies in the review illustrate how cross-level peer teachers try to simplify knowledge by summarizing it to the students (Lockspeiser et al., 2008; Moust & Schmidt, 1994). This learning strategy is significantly different from just reading about a topic or learning to prepare for a test. Other researchers have also found that summarizing can promote deep learning because students are "forced" to find out what content is most important (Fiorella & Mayer, 2016; Roscoe, 2014). For example, in one study from medical school, cross-level peer teachers claimed that they got an opportunity to revise and further develop their knowledge on the subject matter (Evans & Cuffe, 2009). The students must identify the most relevant content so other students are capable of learning about it in an effective way.

Note that summarizing can both be part of lesson preparations and be the lesson itself. In preparing a lesson, the peer teacher will need to select the most relevant information and organize it into a coherent structure. The subject matter must be adapted to a lesson format, whether this is in the form of personal notes or presentation slides. Summarizing happens when students try to make sense of the lesson content, they select by integrating with their prior knowledge. In the first case study, the peer teachers were challenged to select and present the most important content within a topic. They also had to write a short summary of the academic topic. In the comments, some students even highlight the learning value of summarizing the academic content when preparing the lesson. These tasks require a deeper conceptual understanding of the subject matter in order to simplify it in such a way that others can understand it (Fiorella & Mayer, 2016; Roscoe, 2014).

While Aslan (2015) found that students struggled to summarize a topic, one may ask why the students in the first case study did not experience this process as so difficult. One likely explanation is that the students already had good knowledge about the lesson topic since they already had been in the program for one year. In contrast, many of the peer teachers in the second case study experienced that they had to teach about a new topic they were not familiar with. Although the peer teachers received guidance in advance, several of them remarked that they did not have enough background knowledge to offer high-quality lessons.

Additionally, summarizing can be used as a teaching method in wrapping up the actual lesson. It can trigger reflective communication on the subject matter or about the learning objectives (Hattie, 2023). However, in both case studies, there were few such attempts. One reason may be lack of time since the lessons were very short. Another explanation is that peer teachers, especially in the second case study, felt they had inadequate background knowledge, which would have made it difficult to synthesize the student comments.

Learning metacognitive skills

Importantly, peer teacher learning can support the development of metacognitive skills or the ability to reflect on your own learning. Metacognitive regulation involves the ability to plan, monitor, and evaluate one's own learning strategies. It requires awareness and control of one's own cognitive processes. In being better at evaluating the effectiveness of different learning strategies, one can choose more appropriate learning strategies in different settings. Not using the right learning strategies may ultimately lead to poor learning outcomes (Fiorella & Mayer, 2016; Flavell, 1979).

In peer teaching, the metacognitive awareness will manifest itself through the different lesson phases. Compared with other learning activities, the need for an intentional plan will always be required. In the *lesson preparations*, the peer teacher must use assess what strategy can help them find and select the most relevant information. This also requires the ability to accurately evaluate one's own understanding of the material, and how it can be transformed to relevant lesson content.

Equally important, metacognition can play a pivotal role *during the lesson*, particularly in enhancing awareness of the types of communication taking place. Velez et al. (2011) discovered that students engaged in peer teaching exhibited increased metacognitive skills. Such an enhancement bolsters their awareness of their own learning strategies and nuances in interactions with co-teachers and the peer students. Engaging in this kind of reflection can be crucial. It aids educators in discerning the discrepancies between their espoused theory – what they claim to do – and their theory-in-use – what they actually practice in the classroom. For example, both case studies reveal the presence of IRE-communication in whole-class discussions. Notably, in the second case study, only a few peer teachers took the time to expand student comments, pose reflective questions, or provide lesson summaries. (Argyris & Schon, 1992; Parker, 2023).

Furthermore, the *reflection after the lesson* is important in developing metacognitive skills. In metacognition, this ability to evaluate is a core feature. In both case studies, the lesson evaluations offered opportunities to reflect around the learning, but they were directed toward student perception, not direct assessments of what students had learned. In the second case study, the development of metacognitive skills was supported with two written assignments. Each peer teacher group handed in a reflection paper based on peer feedback and teacher feedback after the lesson. This assignment gave the students the opportunity to evaluate the process and reflect on the peer teaching in a more systematic and critical manner.

By using various theories and analytic frameworks, students can adopt alternative perspectives that can produce a deeper understanding (Kolb, 2015, pp. 58–59) and lead to improvements of the lesson in the future. In peer teacher learning, the metacognitive ability will be closely associated with didactical competence, the ability to choose appropriate teaching methods and lesson content. Especially the first case study, a large majority students state they want to implement this pedagogical practice in their own classroom teaching. On the other hand, a relatively large group in the second study were negative toward peer teaching. Some complained that peer teacher learning is too difficult or different from what they were used to. This may also be a consequence of a teaching culture that emphasizes simpler "reproductive" learning strategies.

Acquisition of professional skills

Improving your teaching skills

In collective peer teaching, students gain knowledge about the subject matter and also receive practical teacher training. In both case studies referenced, many students reported an improvement in their teaching proficiency. Similar findings have been reported in other collective peer teaching studies. For instance, in a science teacher education study by Aslan (2015), a majority of peer teachers highlighted their enhanced "vocational competence" as a significant outcome. Furthermore, studies on microteaching, a teaching method akin to collective peer teaching, have reported similar benefits. Such benefits arise because students gain realistic teaching experience and practice (Ralph, 2014).

Importantly, teaching proficiency does not only include skills but also includes the ability to reflect on your own practice (Schön, 1984). In the second case study, most of the students stated that they improved their ability to reflect around their own teaching practice. The written assignments also encouraged students to evaluate the peer lessons, and connect their practical experiences with more general theoretical reflections (Kolb, 2015).

Conversely a relatively large group in the second study did not feel they improved their teaching skills. As previously mentioned, one explanation is that some tasks required very little teaching. Another explanation is that many of these students were not satisfied with the peer feedback. In general, feedback is considered essential in developing professional skills. Expert performance is usually not a function of innate talent but learned from long-term commitment and hard work.

Still, time spent practicing does not automatically lead to learning. High-quality learning involves a particular kind of deliberate practice which involves concentrated, repeated performance that is compared against an ideal or "correct" model of the performance (Ericsson, 2008; Ericsson et al., 1993).

To identify errors, it is necessary with feedback that compares the actual performance against the ideal. In subsequent performances, the person must attempt to correct errors. This work is difficult because it requires focused attention, thoughtful analysis, and continuous repetition to eliminate mistakes and reach goals. The reflection is directed toward a concrete performance and analyzed against a metacognitive ideal model to improve future action in a recurring cycle of learning. Learning relationships are also important because they can provide expert models and emotional support for the focused effort required (Ericsson, 2008; Ericsson et al., 1993; Kolb, 2015, pp. 352–353).

This explains why years of working experience not in itself is a good predictor of performance. Although the peer teachers only are responsible for one lesson, they receive feedback and can potentially use it to improve their practice. The objective is also to provide students with experience in learning from feedback, which can help them when they later participate in professional learning communities in school.

Peer teacher collaboration

Moreover, in both case studies, the students highlighted the learning value of the peer teacher collaboration in teams. A large majority of the students state that they improved their collaborative skills during this work. Likewise, Kobiyashi (2021a) finds stronger learning effects in collaborative preparations compared with individual preparations. Furthermore, the opportunity to teach enable peer teachers to use their creative skills in designing the lesson and when they enact the lesson. Similar positive effects have also been found in microteaching studies.

In a microteaching study by Ralph (2014), the creative work in peer teacher teams is also underscored. This point is mentioned by one student: "Being encouraged to be creative in our group-work added to the team building aspect, and it strengthened our communication and public speaking abilities in front of our peers. I personally enjoyed my involvement in the microteach activities" (Ralph, 2014, p. 23). When students are allowed to be in charge, it is important that they are given freedom to use their creativity.

In the second case study, some student comments even link peer teacher collaboration to the strengthening of the ability to participate in professional learning communities. Although one study in the review (Aslan, 2015) reports that some peer teacher groups found it difficult to plan the lesson together, the co-teaching provides a better opportunity for collective reflection as they can discuss both the subject matter and the instructional strategies. Interestingly, Martin (2018) finds that close collaboration through demanding preparations can often improve relations between peer teachers. It suggests that co-teaching can be a way of strengthening interpersonal relations among students because the student group must both plan and lead a lesson together.

Together, these empirical findings suggest that campus in teacher education can be used as a context for practice-based learning.

Peer teacher motivation

Social responsibility and performance anxiety

Numerous studies in the review indicate that students are motivated in the role of a peer teacher, both at the same-level (Aslan, 2015, 2017a, 2017b; Velez et al., 2011) and in cross-level peer teaching (Lockspeiser et al., 2008). For instance, in the study by Aslan (2015), 73% (30 out of 41) of students had a positive attitude toward learning by teaching as a method in teacher education. Martin (2018) also emphasizes that strong student motivation is a fundamental feature of collective peer teaching. In the first case study, most students were motivated, while motivation was mixed in the second case study. Only one-third of students were highly motivated for peer teaching, while as many as 40% of students were not motivated at all.

Exploring the reasons behind the positive motivation, both case studies revealed that the responsibility for others' learning was significant. In the role of a peer teacher, learning about the subject matter transcends personal importance. Particularly, students in the first case study assert that they invested considerable effort in the lesson preparations, describing it as a profound learning process. Similarly, a study in the review finds that second-year peer teachers in medical education report a strong sense of duty in assisting first-year students (Lockspeiser et al., 2008).

Moreover, students can be motivated by an "audience effect" or by assuming the most powerful role in the classroom. Puchner (2003) emphasizes that stepping into the role of a peer teacher involves adopting a teacher's characteristics, including status, authority, attitudes, and responsibility. In "same-level" collective peer teaching, all students have the opportunity to take charge, which some may find highly motivating.

On the other hand, both case studies indicate that performance anxiety often accompanies feelings of social responsibility. For instance, in the first case study, some students found it difficult to concentrate on others' teaching because they were highly focused on their own lesson preparations. This issue is less prevalent when peer lessons are distributed throughout the term, as in the second case study. However, 20% of students in this study reported a very high level of performance anxiety and significantly higher stress levels compared to teaching children in school. Some students noted that the responsibility of leading most of the lessons was overwhelming. With fewer faculty-led lectures, the peer lessons became even more critical, escalating the pressure to deliver a good lesson. Additionally, there was a pervasive "fear of failing," marked by a desire to avoid the embarrassment of not being able to answer a question in front of the students, which often resulted in brief whole-class discussions. As many as 29% of the students did not enjoy leading the whole-class discussions.[1]

Mastery of the lesson

Despite this, peer teacher learning often strengthened students' professional confidence. Although a large group of students in the second case study had low motivation, around half of the students still experienced a strong degree of mastery after having completed the lesson. Even among those students who experienced a lot of stress, half of them felt either a moderate or strong degree of mastery after the lesson was completed. Table 5.1 provides an overview of the statistical relationship between perceived stress and the sense of accomplishment after completing the lesson.

Table 5.1 Relationship between degree of stress and degree of accomplishment in peer teaching (percentage frequency distribution)

(N = 88)	Little degree of accomplishment after the lesson	Moderate degree of accomplishment	Strong degree of accomplishment	Total (N)
Much more stressful to stand in front of peers than in front of students	41%	23%	36%	100% (22)
Slightly more stressful to stand in front of peers than in front of students	11%	40%	49%	100% (45)
About the same in terms of stress level	5%	52%	43%	100% (21)

Even among those students who experienced a lot of stress compared with teaching in schools, half of the students felt either a moderate or strong degree of mastery after the lesson. It illustrates that a high level of performance anxiety may not necessarily be negative if students can cope with it.

According to Duran and Topping (2017), a certain degree of stress can have a positive influence on motivation. For instance, in one peer teaching study, a peer teacher states, "I liked that I took the place of the teacher. It was a little bit frightening, but it was a great honor to teach my schoolmates" (Tsevreni, 2018, p. 75). Here, feelings of pride are closely linked to fear. The word "honor" indicates that the peer teacher felt they were important when they were assigned to be responsible for a whole lesson. At the same time the phrase "a little bit frightening" indicates the presence of performance anxiety and possibly a fear of failing. It follows that the pleasure of teaching can to some degree also involve performance anxiety. Instead, it becomes more important that the level of anxiety is within an acceptable level, stimulating the lesson to become a "flow experience" (Csikszentmihalyi, 1990).

Other researchers also claim peer teachers can improve their self-confidence and communication competence (Topping et al., 2017, p. 22). By being able to successfully complete such a lesson, this student felt a sense of achievement. Peer teachers can experience a sense of fulfillment from teaching (Lockspeiser et al., 2008). Mastering difficult or unexpected teaching challenges can strengthen students' professional self-confidence. In teacher education, one can argue that it is important that students learn how to cope with difficult challenges, cope with anxiety and develop resilience.

Peer teacher interests

If peer teachers lack relevant subject matter knowledge, this threatens the quality of the peer teaching. In same-level collective peer teaching, they will need to acquire a good understanding during the course before they have the lesson. If the motivation in the lesson preparations is low, the likely result is teaching of low quality. This becomes not only a problem for the student who is a peer teacher, but also for the whole class.

Therefore, it is essential that the individuals are motivated to invest enough cognitive effort in trying to grasp the material. To strengthen motivation, one important design strategy is to build on peer teacher interests. This can be done by both allowing free choice of lesson content and teaching methods. This will also allow students to utilize more of their unique background knowledge.

If teaching does not engage students' prior knowledge, they will often just learn the material well enough to pass the test (Sawyer, 2022). Within constructivism, any effort to teach should be connected to learner's prior knowledge and preconceptions (Hein, 1991).

If we look at the student interest in the subject matter in the two case studies, they were quite different . In the first case study, the peer teachers were allowed to freely choose one among 42 different topics. This strengthened the intrinsic motivation. Students were also given approximately one month to prepare a lesson, allowing more reading time. With increased background knowledge about the subject matter, students are likely to be more confident about the lesson. In addition, students could choose whom to collaborate with, assuming they would find somebody with a similar interest. Interestingly, these students did not receive any guidance in advance. It appears that their freedom to choose lesson content was enough to make them confident and give them a feeling of control over the situation. Few peer teachers reported about performance anxiety or a lack of sufficient background knowledge.

Conversely, in the second peer teaching design, the free choice opportunities were limited. The students were instead assigned to teach different topics. Some were even given specific assignments that deviated significantly from the rest of the group, which increased the perceptions of unfairness.

Consequently, a relatively large group of peer teachers stated that they were not interested in the lesson content they had to teach others. This made them less enthusiastic about their own teaching.

Although the second peer teaching design offered a pre-mentoring session, this did not help all students in gaining interest in the subject matter. With the short preparation time of one week, one can also question whether the peer teachers had enough time to develop an interest in the subject matter. Several student comments point to the use of minimum strategies in their lesson preparations. This lack of knowledge about the subject matter may also have increased the nervousness during the lesson. Students will avoid situations they think might embarrass them in front of the whole class, like leading whole-class discussions on an advanced academic level.

Motivation and formal assessment

Another motivational factor is the formal assessment. In general, motivation is reliant on the learner acknowledging the reasons why it is necessary to learn something. With some students, relevance for the exam is a very important motivational factor. In both case studies, the peer teaching was a mandatory assignment that all students had to do, but it was not graded. In the first study, the peer teachers might have had a stronger extrinsic motivation because the peer teaching performance was labeled as a "mid-way exam." In addition, all students completed the lesson within a short period of just a few days which may have strengthened the feeling of taking an exam. Still, most students perceived their level of performance anxiety as acceptable.

In contrast, the peer teaching in the second study was spread over the whole semester. All the other mandatory assignments also made it more tempting to use less time on the peer teaching assignment. These students also felt the link to the formal assessment was weaker. For example, one-third of the students think the whole course should have focused more on the syllabus and the exam. This is likely to have reduced the peer teacher motivation.

Iterative learning

One of the most distinctive features of peer teacher learning is its cyclical learning method. This process develops through several unique yet interconnected stages. A key aspect of these stages is that they all require revisiting the same topic multiple times. The first stage is centered around planning and preparing the lesson, the second stage focuses on delivering the lesson and interacting with students, while the third stage is about reflecting on and evaluating the lesson. Unlike cross-level peer teachers who typically manage multiple lessons, those involved in collective peer teaching usually handle only a single lesson. As a result, they only go through a single cycle of peer teacher learning during a course. The following sections provide a more in-depth discussion of these three stages.

Preparation phase

The initial phase involves the learning that occurs as peer teachers develop their lesson plans. In the context of collective peer teaching, these teachers often require more preparation time due to unfamiliarity with the material. The level of learning achieved varies, influenced by both the duration of the preparation stage and the effort exerted during this time. For instance, in the first case study, the peer teachers were allocated significantly more preparation time compared to the second case study, and they reported putting additional effort into their preparations.

This phase typically involves substantial individual literature review, information gathering, and note-taking. These tasks are driven by a clear objective: determining the most relevant content for the lesson. Within a set timeframe, the syllabus's subject matter needs to be converted into pertinent lesson content and instructional material. Even cross-level peer teachers, who have recently finished the course, generally require some preparation time to accomplish this (Duran & Topping, 2017). Multiple peer teaching studies have reported learning improvements during this stage (Bargh & Schul, 1980; Benware & Deci, 1984; Kobayashi, 2019; Topping et al., 2017). In terms of emotions, the social obligation of aiding others' learning plays a crucial role. It generates a more genuine motivation but also increases stress and performance anxiety, particularly if insufficient time is provided for preparation.

Enactment phase

The second phase pertains to the learning that peer teachers acquire during the actual lesson. The enactment phase encompasses a variety of learning tasks, such as explaining the material, engaging with the group by responding to queries, and summarizing the lesson. When explaining, peer teachers often enhance their academic learning if they articulate their thoughts about the lesson content, instead of merely parroting the syllabus or reading from their notes (Fiorella & Mayer, 2016). Both approaches were observed in the case studies, indicating that this issue should be addressed during pre-mentoring sessions.

Moreover, peer teachers are encouraged to respond to students' inquiries or stimulate whole-class discussions aimed at achieving collective comprehension. This can trigger further elaboration on the lesson content and promote introspection about one's understanding. The caliber of these reflections will depend on both the questions asked and how the peer teacher handles them (Duran, 2017; Fiorella & Mayer, 2016). Even though peer teachers in both case studies typically posed a few reflective queries to the student group, the subsequent full-group discussions and teacher responses were often brief.

It's important to note that peer teacher learning also involves physical interaction with students. This might include activities such as writing on the blackboard or highlighting information on visual aids within the classroom. Some refer to this as "learning by doing" or "learning by enacting" (Fiorella & Mayer, 2016). This form of embodied learning was particularly noticeable when some peer teachers participated in role-play for their fellow students during the museum tour.

Emotionally, the process of lesson enactment can elicit a positive sense of mindfulness and heightened awareness of one's surroundings. However, there is a potential downside: anxiety may take over, and student inquiries may seem intimidating.

Post-lesson phase

The third phase, following the lesson, involves the peer teacher reflecting on the events of the lesson, either through personal recollection or feedback from others. Formal feedback from the teacher was a crucial component in both case studies. Similar to the study by Velez et al. (2011), the peer teachers found this feedback valuable. However, opinions about peer feedback were more varied. In the first case study, most students reacted positively, but in the second, a considerable number felt they didn't gain much from it. This brings up the issue of whether students are adequately trained to provide feedback to each other.

Crucially, the post-lesson stage should allow peer teachers to evaluate whether it's necessary to adjust the current lesson or their comprehension of the subject matter (Duran & Topping, 2017). Although students in collective peer teaching won't teach the same material again, they can still be assigned tasks that foster this kind of reflection. In the second case study, the peer teachers wrote a reflection paper based on the feedback they received. They also wrote an individual reflection on this topic in their semester paper. This third round of learning can lead to a deeper understanding of the subject matter, improve teaching performance, and further understanding of peer teaching as a teaching method. With regard to emotions after the lesson, the data suggest that most peer teachers moved from feelings of nervousness and anxiety to a sense of accomplishment, pride, and success. Conversely, a small proportion of students didn't enjoy the teaching experience, a concern that needs to be addressed in this post-lesson stage. Table 5.2 provides an overview of the basic characteristics of the iterative learning process in peer teacher learning.

Recognizing the distinct and interconnected functions of each stage in this learning process is crucial. The case studies demonstrate that peer teachers experience intense emotions that shift through the phases. Anxiety is prevalent during both the preparation and enactment phases, while relief and a sense of mastery dominate the post-lesson phase.

Summarization serves as an example of a learning strategy that is valuable across all stages. In the preparation phase, the peer teacher must identify the most pertinent content for the lesson. During the lesson enactment, this material should be distilled and conveyed by the peer teachers in their own words. Additionally, the peer teacher can try to summarize ongoing discussions or the entire lesson alongside the students during the lesson. This sort of teacher training offers a chance to hone teaching methods that can promote in-depth learning. In the post-lesson phase, identifying the key points of the lesson becomes crucial. One instance of this was seen in the first case study, where students were asked to submit a written summary of the lesson content.

Table 5.2 The three phases of peer teacher learning

Dimension in deep learning	1. Preparation phase: lesson planning (preparations)	2. Enactment phase: lesson enactment (learning by enacting)	3. Post-lesson phase: lesson evaluation
Feelings	- Social responsibility for others learning (authentic motivation) vs performance anxiety (fear of failing) - Self-confidence - Interest in the subject matter	- Mindfulness (culmination of preparation) vs nervousness (not being able to answer questions from students) - Enjoyment vs boredom	- Mastery vs frustration - Pride vs disappointment
Explaining	- Explaining to others (peer teacher team) - Self-explaining (alone)	- Explaining to others (recitation vs improvisation) - Asking reflective questions ("knowledge telling" vs "knowledge building")	- Metacognition (reflection around the lesson) - Evaluating the lesson with others ("thinking aloud")
Embodied cognition	- Learning by drawing	- Learning by drawing - Learning by enacting	
Reflective questions	- Asking and answering questions in the peer teacher team. If done alone, self-questioning is relevant	- Asking and answering questions in the student group - IRE communication vs dialogical interaction	- Asking answering questions about the lesson in the peer teacher group, either with colleagues or with students. (If done alone, self-questioning is relevant.)
Summarizing	- Summarizing the most relevant lesson content	- Summarizing the subject matter or discussions in class	- Summarizing key aspects of the lesson that need improvement
Mode of reflection	- Written reflection-on action	- Verbal reflection-in-action	- Written or verbal reflection-on-action
Acquisition of professional skills	- Learning how to prepare a lesson	- Learning how to enact a lesson	- Learning how to evaluate a lesson

Moving through different modes of reflection

The iterative learning process moves through various forms of reflection. According to Schön (1984), reflective practitioners partake in an ongoing cycle of reflection, learning, and adjustment. There are primarily two modes of reflection. The first, reflection-in-action, happens during the actual practice, where professionals consider their actions while executing them. They question, assess, and modify their actions in real time to better react to the unique situations and unexpected issues they encounter. The second, reflection-on-action, occurs after the event has transpired. Professionals dissect what occurred and enhance their comprehension of their practice. They also contemplate alternative actions they might have taken and devise new strategies for future scenarios. By engaging in reflection, practitioners can refine their professional expertise.

Considering the iterative learning process, the lesson enactment phase corresponds to reflection-in-action. This is a more spontaneous form of reflection, primarily verbal. The reflection during the lesson enactment will be markedly different. The timeframe is brief, and the peer teacher often has to respond immediately to unexpected queries. The lesson plan may also need to be adapted during the lesson, requiring on-the-spot adjustments based on classroom interactions.

This phase can also be seen as a second round of learning, where the subject matter transitions from more "tacit" written reflections during the preparation phase to verbal reflections in the lesson. The pace of reflection is different in the enactment phase. It's more immediate, differing from the deliberate and written reflection prior to the lesson. Nevertheless, the peer teacher must continually assess whether to adhere to the original lesson plan.

Additionally, the lesson preparation phase and the post-evaluation phase align with what Schön describes as reflection-on-action. However, the pace of reflection varies when comparing different lesson preparations. In the preparation phase, the upcoming lesson provides the final deadline that frames this period. The sense of urgency will differ based on the instructional design. In the first case study, peer teachers had a few months to prepare, while in the second case study, students had about a week. This establishes different opportunities to gain relevant knowledge with varying degrees of time pressure.

In the third phase, after the lesson, the peer teacher will evaluate what transpired and consider what could have been done differently. In theory, there is no time limit here since the peer teacher isn't preparing a new lesson. Here, time pressure will usually be associated with deadlines for submitting assignments related to reflections on the lesson. However, the events are easier to recall if reflection happens shortly after. Sometimes there are evaluation meetings with classmates as well.

Together, these three distinct forms of reflection provide both repetition and variation in the learning process. The repeated engagement with the same topic isn't merely repetitive, but further elaboration on the same subject in different ways. Additionally, students practice their professional teaching skills in all three phases, learning how to plan and evaluate a lesson. They also gain insights into peer teaching as a pedagogical practice, and the written assignments encourage deeper reflection on this subject.

Summary—peer teacher learning as deep learning

This section has shown how peer teacher learning involves the use of higher-order thinking skills, the acquirement of professional skills, learning cycle, and a more socially orientated motivation. In combination, these characteristics fit well with many definitions of deep learning (Sawyer, 2022). In recent years, the notion of deep learning has received more attention and has typically been linked to 21st-century skills and future skills which the society needs. The concept has been integrated in the curriculum all over the world, also in Norway.

First, metacognition is usually described as an important part of deep learning. Students learn better when they express their developing knowledge and reflectively analyze it—either through conversation, by writing texts, or creating artifacts. In contrast, surface learning let learners memorize facts or carry out procedures without understanding how or why. The lesson content is treated as static knowledge (Sawyer, 2022).

As previously mentioned, metacognitive skills are an important part of peer teacher learning. Many strategic decisions must be made about the subject matter. In planning a lesson, one must decide how to acquire an understanding of topic and how to make it relevant to other students learning needs. In this way, the metacognition is to some degree "externalized" because the others learning is what motivate the strategic decisions about your own learning. However, because of the motivation to do a good lesson, the peer teacher will typically need to decide how one can acquire a deep understanding of the subject matter within a limited period. Notably, in co-teacher collaboration, a significant part of the metacognition will be transformed into verbal meta-communication because reflections on the lesson content and the learning process will happen through discussions with other peer teachers.

Second, deep learning is often associated with authentic problem-solving processes encouraging students to identify, analyze, and address complex, real-world problems. The learning experiences should be relevant to student lives, interests, and later professional work. When students gain a deeper conceptual understanding, they learn facts and procedures in a more useful way by knowing which situations to apply it in and how to modify it for each new situation (Sawyer, 2022).

In peer teacher learning, the learning process does not only involve academic learning, but the development of a wide range of other professional skills. Teacher training involves all three phases of teaching: preparation, enactment, and evaluation. The peer teachers are challenged to integrate their personal and practical experiences in the teaching. Especially the lesson enactment requires peer teacher apply their knowledge about the subject matter, modifying and adapting it can meet student learning needs in the most effective way. On top of that, peer teachers can gain self-confidence by receiving recognition from other students and through mastering the teaching challenges.

Besides this, peer teacher learning can be regarded as an authentic problem-solving because it centers on the responsibility for others learning. Building on the basic human motivation to help others (Baltzersen, 2022, pp. 265–266). it can be regarded as a specific type of growth motivation (Maslow, 1981). In constructivism, learning is also described as a social activity that includes both persons we know and unknown others. Referring to John Dewey, Hein (1991) criticizes traditional education because it tends to isolate the learner from all social interaction, emphasizing a one-on-one relationship between the learner and the objective material to be learned. Instead, education should involve conversation, interaction with others, and the opportunity to use knowledge. Peer teacher learning fits well into this line of thought with its emphasis on social learning processes.

Third, deep learning acknowledges the diverse needs, interests, and learning styles of students and strives to adjust the learning to these individual experiences. It requires that students actively participate in their own learning, preferably being in a learning environment that builds on student existing knowledge and interests (Sawyer, 2022).

Similarly, in peer teacher learning it is important to build on student interests. In addition, the peer teachers will switch on constructing their own learning environment by organizing the different peer lessons.

Fourth, deep learning takes time. According to Hein (1991), one principle in constructivist learning is that "It takes time to learn." It is necessary to revisit ideas: try, reflect, and use them. Learning doesn't happen instantaneous but is usually a product of repeated exposure and thought to the same content or skills. Deep insight will typically build require longer periods of preparation and is very difficult to achieve without enough time (Hein, 1991).

Likewise, in peer teacher learning, it takes time to moving through all phases in the iterative learning processes. Obviously, the length of all phases will influence to what degree deep conceptual understanding is obtainable.

Fifth, deep learning requires that learners look for patterns and underlying principles. Learners should evaluate new ideas critically, synthesize information, and relate them to conclusions. It emphasizes that students develop a conceptual understanding of the subject matter, rather than simply memorizing facts or procedures. This understanding enables students to apply their knowledge to novel situations and transfer their learning across different domains (Sawyer, 2022).

In peer teacher learning, all the student work is centered around one problem, the "construction" of a lesson which requires extensive work on one topic. In preparing a lesson, students will seek to select the most relevant lesson content, which motivates them to seek a deep conceptual understanding of the core structure in the academic content. The iterative learning spurs reflection in several rounds. During the lesson, peer teachers must both explain the lesson content and engage in it together with others. After the lesson, the peer teacher will usually evaluate the relevance of the selected lesson content. This is not simple repetition, but a deep learning process involving a wide range of learning activities. It has the potential to positively transform attitudes toward the subject matter.

Note

1 See the Appendix, *Table 9.8* Student perceptions of peer teacher learning.

6 Perspectives on peer student learning

Introduction

This chapter will discuss peer student learning, one of three learning positions in collective peer teaching. Especially the first case study shows that peer student learning can be perceived to be of very high quality. In cross-level peer teaching too, several studies have shown how these lessons can be of very high quality. For instance, in one study of anatomy teaching in medical school, students perceived no differences in academic level between experienced fourth-year peer teachers and the senior staff (Evans & Cuffe, 2009). The other cross-level peer teaching studies also find that the quality of the peer teaching is equal to the faculty-led teaching (Lockspeiser et al., 2008; Moust & Schmidt, 1994). This is perhaps not surprising when we know these peer teachers have passed the exam and just recently gone through the learning process.

In comparison, when all students at the same level are assigned to be teachers for each other, there is a strong fear that the quality of the academic learning may be substantially impoverished (Duran Gisbert & Monereo Font, 2008). Some of the collective peer teaching studies in the review also show that students are more skeptical toward the academic quality. For example, in the study by Aslan (2015), teacher guidance before the lesson is considered essential in avoiding misconceptions and optimizing lesson quality. This makes these results even more surprising since the students did not receive any guidance from the faculty teacher in their preparations.

Although perceived learning is not actual learning, the positive findings indicate that collective peer teaching can have a transformative potential. Still, the quantitative findings reveal a paradox. The very reason the students follow a course is because they have inadequate knowledge which it is assumed that the formal teacher possesses. On the one hand, one can dismiss the empirical findings in the present study as a "lucky" one-time incident. Since the results build on student perceptions, student opinions can obviously be biased, and they might exaggerate the learning benefits of the peer teaching.

On the other hand, these "counterintuitive" results may have revealed something important about learning that we do not fully understand. Do the students possess a different kind of knowledge, do they select different lesson content, use other teaching methods, or are they more engaged in the teaching? Findings in both case studies display some of the characteristics in this type of learning. In this section, the type of learning will be further discussed in relation to the lesson content, the assessment, the classroom interaction, and how engaging the teaching is.

Relevant lesson content

One important feature with the lesson content is how it seeks to bridge theoretical and practical knowledge. For example, most students in the second case study claim they improved their ability to reflect on their (teaching) practice. However, several students also criticized the peer lessons for their lack of theoretical perspectives. Several lessons were primarily organized around the sharing of their own practical experiences with few links to theoretical knowledge. Some peer teachers did not present academic concepts in a thorough way, and discussions became too informal, dominated by everyday language. Although there are advantages with peer teachers speaking the same language as the students (Moust & Schmidt, 1994; Velez et al., 2011), there is a risk that this language restricts the reflections. In addition, the formal teacher had little time to comment on the lesson content afterward the peer lessons. On top of that, the students were offered few faculty-led lectures which could have challenged students' practical knowledge and created a better mix of lessons.

Consequently, students in the second case study were uncertain about the relevance of the lesson content and the peer teacher explanations, especially in relation to the summative assessment. In contrast to cross-level peer teaching, trustworthiness will be a core issue in "same-level" collective peer teaching. Misconceptions will be more present and can make the learning process messier than what the students are used to in faculty teaching. Likewise, in a similar collective peer teaching design, Aslan (2015) found that two-thirds of the peer students mentioned misconceptions as one of the most important disadvantages. Several students in this study expressed that the faculty teachers could have offered a better academic introduction to the topic. In a similar manner, the problem with the peer teaching design in the second case study was that a small group of students were entirely responsible for the lesson each week. Often, these peer teachers were not familiar with the subject matter in advance, and they also lacked interest in the lesson content motivation.

Conversely, students do not mention the lack of theoretical perspectives as a problem in the first peer teaching design. Students report of a surprisingly high level of academic learning and no lack of trust. As previously mentioned, many students even perceived the peer teaching to be better than the faculty teaching. One explanation is that these peer teachers would always do a theoretical presentation, which often aimed to merge the explanation of scientific concepts with practical experiences. These peer teachers had significant teaching experience from school and could therefore utilize more of their practical knowledge.

In the teacher education context, one of the most important differences between a peer teacher and a faculty teacher is the proximity to the practical experiences. One important advantage with using peer teachers is that they can introduce interesting examples, dilemmas, or professional challenges that are both personal and authentic. On the one hand, this peer lesson can offer more relevant lessons through the narratives. As argued by Bruner (1991), we organize our experience and our memory of human happenings mainly in the form of stories and myths. This type of teaching can strengthen student engagement. However, when there is uncertainty regarding the academic level of the peer teaching, it needs to be properly balanced with faculty teaching.

On the other hand, this type of peer lesson can be designed as problem-based learning. If peer teachers have sufficient practical and theoretical knowledge, they can be effective in finding the right cognitive level to engage the student by anticipating the problems students typically will struggle with. They can be better at identifying what the students do not yet understand. In this way, the lesson content will be perceived as less distant and more connected to the specific educational setting.

Many studies of cross-level peer teaching have found that peer explanations can serve as a valuable supplement to teacher explanations because they are different, but still relevant (Evans & Cuffe, 2009; Loda et al., 2019; Rees et al., 2016; Stigmar, 2016; Topping et al., 2017). These peer teachers are more sensitive toward the matters they typically struggle with, and they will also have sufficient theoretical knowledge because they have already completed the course. Under some circumstances, peer teachers may also be able to address the theoretical knowledge at an appropriate level of complexity. For example, in one study in the review, students complain that some faculty professors who are very familiar with academic concepts may have difficulties translating this knowledge into language which the student understands. In contrast, a peer teacher will still know more than the student group but use a more similar language and be closer to the problem-solving process.

However, with same-level peer teachers, the level of theoretical background knowledge is not certain in the same way. Regarding this group, an important question is to identify the minimum level of theoretical knowledge a peer teacher needs to do a good lesson. Surprisingly, in the first case study the teacher educator did not guide the students in the lesson preparation phase. Still, the students perceived the quality of teaching as high. One explanation is that some students chose topics they had already learned about during the first year of the program, while the others could choose a lesson topic of their own interest. These factors appear to be more important than receiving guidance from the formal teacher in advance.

Regarding faculty teaching, some teacher educators may also lack sufficient practical knowledge, have little teaching experience or interest in what happens in schools. Then, there is a risk that the lesson content is too orientated toward theoretical knowledge. In this sense, peer teachers may offer valuable supplementary perspectives by utilizing practical knowledge that faculty staff may be lacking. In addition, the peer teachers can also be more interested in the students. Studies of cross-level peer teaching show that the peer teacher is often orientated toward student learning in a more holistic perspective, addressing both the social and academic life as a student. The teacher support is more directed toward peer students' needs, difficulties, and expectations, which can potentially reduce their anxiety. Because the peer teachers have recently completed the same course, they have been in a more similar life situation and can remember the feelings they are taking the course (Loda et al., 2019; Rees et al., 2016).

Relevance for the summative assessment

Studies in higher education show that students adapt their student behavior and learning strategies to the assessment system (Harlen et al., 2002). Therefore, one important question is how peer student learning is influenced by the formal assessment system.

Regarding the summative assessment in the course, the two case studies were relevant in different ways. In the first case study, the complete peer teaching arrangement was organized as a "mid-way exam" in the course. This increased the motivation to do a good lesson even when the students knew it was easy to pass. In addition, all peer teacher teams were assigned to provide summaries of the lesson content which were shared in the whole class. The result was an aggregated pool of digital material which was very relevant for the second-year final exam.

In the second case study, a relatively large group did not think that the peer lessons were relevant for the semester paper. A fundamental challenge in same-level collective peer teaching, is that the peer students will be more uncertain whether the teaching of the subject matter is relevant for the summative assessment. Nor was the connection clearly described by the formal teachers. If students are allowed to choose content according to their interests, it may be perceived as relevant for the exam.

Conversely, in cross-level peer teaching, there will be much fewer concerns about the lesson content because the peer teachers are qualified by having completed the course. Peer teachers will usually talk about the exam because they have just recently completed the course and have the exam fresh in mind. These peer teachers find satisfaction in sharing what they have recently learned and how they acquired the subject matter in a successful way (Topping et al., 2017). Although these peer teachers do not have as much of the expertise as the faculty staff, they are more able to anticipate how the learning process will unfold. This can make them more sensitive toward the student learning needs and concepts students are struggling to understand (Lockspeiser et al., 2008). As a result, the lesson content will usually be presented together with reflection around the problem-solving processes, the learning strategies, and the personal learning story. The lesson will not only be about what content, concepts, or problems that are most relevant, but it may also be explicit discussions of effective learning strategies. Because these peer teachers have recently gone through the learning process, they will remember their learning challenges and why it was difficult to understand a concept or develop a skill. Students who aim to get a good grade will look at the peer teachers as role models. This can potentially also strengthen students´ metacognitive abilities.

However, because the peer teachers in the two case studies were at the same level, there was less emphasis on how the lessons were relevant for the final summative assessment. From a learning perspective, the advantage is less risk of a too instrumental and exam-orientated pedagogical practice that only emphasizes "teaching to the test." On the other hand, it may become more important that the formal teacher helps connect peer-produced lesson content to the summative assessment.

Whole-class discussions (dialogic teaching)

Concerning the classroom interaction, most of the peer lessons in both case studies were characterized by a presentation that introduced a topic which afterward was followed up with some kind of group work. There was often little time left for whole-class discussions and few challenging questions were posed. Few studies have examined if peer teachers' explanations can be beneficial to students' learning. One exception is Roscoe (2014) who finds that peer students' learning gains were positively correlated with the frequency of knowledge-building explanations provided by the peer teachers. However, this study did not distinguish between peer teachers initial-explanation, where peer students acted as mere listeners and the interaction phases between peer teachers and peer students. In a more recent study, results suggest that both the initial-explanation and interaction phases contribute to learning by teaching face-to-face (Kobayashi, 2021b)

Especially in the second case study, both peer teachers and students even appeared to avoid the interaction phase. Whole-class discussions were often dominated by IRE communication (Cazden, 2001). Although the teacher educators encouraged other types of classroom talk, there were few follow-up questions or elaborations around student comments. One explanation may be that the peer teachers lack training in other types of classroom discourse. Other studies have also found that peer teachers risk providing unsatisfactory explanations and pose questions to the student group which are too shallow and limited in the level of cognitive demand (Topping et al., 2017). In teacher education, a key question is if student teachers need more teacher training on campus to strengthen their ability to facilitate classroom discussions.

Another explanation is that several peer teachers were uncertain about their own level of background knowledge, thus wanting to avoid a situation where they could not answer a question in front of their peers. Especially in one of the seminar groups, many students felt that the classroom atmosphere was not good. Other peer teaching studies emphasize that a trusting peer relationship makes it easier to discuss misconceptions or do corrections openly in class. Peer students will participate more if they feel free to ask questions and give feedback (Loda et al., 2019).

Engaging teaching (other teaching methods)

Concerning engaging teaching, the first case study shows that the students were more enthusiastic about the peer lesson than in the ordinary lectures. The lessons were perceived to be engaging and fun. The peer teachers were allowed to freely choose teaching methods and lesson content. As a result, the peer teacher used various teaching methods, also inspired by their work as teachers in school. Likewise, other studies have found that peer teachers are able to design more engaging lessons than faculty teachers. Because they have a similar background, they tend to know what teaching methods are engaging. They also use a similar humor and are often more enthusiastic about the teaching (Lockspeiser et al., 2008; Moust & Schmidt, 1994; Velez et al., 2011).

Conversely, in the second case study, a relatively large group of peer students did not experience the lessons as engaging. Although the peer teachers could choose their own teaching methods, they could not choose lesson content according to their own interests. This appears to have reduced the teacher enthusiasm. These findings illustrate that peer teaching does not automatically lead to more engaging teaching, but it depends on whether peer teachers are allowed to be creative and utilize their personal and practical experiences in a successful way.

Proximity as the fundamental characteristic of peer student learning?

In addressing peer student learning, it is important to elaborate on the terms that are theoretically relevant. In two of the studies in the qualitative review, the term congruence is used to explain how the learning processes in peer teaching differ from faculty teaching (Lockspeiser et al., 2008; Moust & Schmidt, 1994).

Other more recent studies have also used congruence as a term to describe the peer student learning (Loda et al., 2019). Here, the qualities in the learning process are connected to different types of increased proximity. Although these studies do not provide any detailed explanation of the term and its mechanisms (Moust & Schmidt, 1994), it is common to distinguish between cognitive and social congruence (Lockspeiser et al., 2008; Loda et al., 2019). On the one hand, "cognitive congruence" is orientated toward the subject matter and address how peer teachers and peer students have a more similar level of academic background knowledge. In comparison with faculty teachers, it is proposed that this can make it easier for peer teachers to teach at a more appropriate level (Lockspeiser et al., 2008; Loda et al., 2019; Rees et al., 2016; Stigmar, 2016; Topping et al., 2017). In constructivism too, finding the right level to engage the learner is regarded as one of the most important learning challenges (Hein, 1991). Thus, cognitive congruence will address both design questions, both regarding the selection of the subject matter and the teaching methods.

On the other hand, the term "social congruence" is oriented toward the student and describes how peer teachers and peer students share the same social background. This similarity often makes peer teachers better able to understand and empathize with student learning needs. This includes their emotional difficulties in the course and how they cope with life as a student. Consequently, peer teachers will typically engage in a more symmetrical and informal relationship with the students (Loda et al., 2019).

It is evident that there needs to be some level of congruence between student and teacher in all teaching. Compared to faculty teaching, peer teaching can strengthen this congruence, but how important is it for learning? From a theoretical perspective, congruence as a term is closely linked to the notion of a zone of proximate development (ZPD). In their book about learning by teaching, Duran and Topping (2017) also highlight the ZPD more specifically. The ZPD describes the space between what one can learn alone and what one can do with the help of others. This support must be given within a certain range of proximity. The mediator can either be a teacher or a peer but will need to be aware of the level of actual development and how it can be further developed. Individuals learn when they move beyond their present knowledge, but only within a certain range. For example, explanations that are too difficult to understand will fall outside the zone. Ideally, teachers need to identify the necessary minimum support and gradually withdraw the support, so students can do the learning on their own (Duran & Topping, 2017).

Although congruence can be linked to the ZPD, it is still unclear what the ideal distance is. When is the teacher within the zone or outside of it? Although Vygotsky does not distinguish between different types of proximity in the zone, the analysis of peer teaching suggests that this is possible. Table 6.1 provides an overview of the characteristics of what can be labeled as a zone of cognitive and social proximity within peer student learning as a learning position.

Table 6.1 Characteristics of a zone of cognitive and social proximity in peer student learning: an overview

Peer student learning in the zone of cognitive proximity	Peer student learning in the zone of social proximity
- More relevant lesson content (e.g. other examples like more practical knowledge from school). - More aware of students learning needs (finding the right cognitive level to engage the learner). - More focus on the learning process (learning strategies). - More focus on "peer teacher learning history as a student." (Proximity to the problem-solving process.) - Anticipate the problems students will struggle with. - Uncertainty around the answers (reduced academic trustworthiness—students become more critical). - More emphasis on providing an overview of the subject matter. - More emphasis on exam preparations (a stronger emphasis on "teaching to the test"). - Speaking a more similar academic language.	- More symmetrical group relationship. - More engaging and fun teaching. - More enthusiastic teachers. - More spontaneous and informal learning environment. More positive climate. - More similar humor. - More "free speech" in whole-class discussions (Classroom interaction). - Showing more emotional support and empathy with student life situation.

The zone of cognitive proximity

First, *the zone of cognitive proximity* is orientated toward the academic learning of the subject matter. The main concern about peer student learning will usually be if the theoretical knowledge acquisition is of sufficient high quality. In the teacher education context, it is important to find the right balance between theoretical and practical knowledge acquisition. In contrast to faculty teachers, peer teachers can integrate the lesson content with more recent practical and personal teaching experiences in the lesson content. The empirical findings also show that students were encouraged to reflect on their practice. In contrast, faculty teachers may either lack recent practical experiences or they will be far back in time.

Furthermore, the vocabulary and selection of examples are often more appropriate to the age and cultural background of the students (Duran & Topping, 2017). The more informal academic language can potentially offer better explanations, which are not too advanced, nor too simple. However, the increase in academic "uncertainty" can make students more critical toward proposed answers or solutions. It raises the question of the learning value of misconceptions. Is it always best that the teacher provides answers or explanations that are automatically perceived as correct?

On the other hand, peer teachers can introduce personal experiences in their lessons which can strengthen the trustworthiness or meaningfulness of the lesson content. This may sometimes lead them to be better able to explain concepts at an appropriate level because the peer students are more familiar with the language. Therefore, the peer teacher perspective on the subject matter can offer a stronger focus on the practical knowledge acquisition.

A key question regarding cognitive proximity is how much more academic background knowledge a teacher should have compared with the student. Can teacher explanations be too advanced? Who can provide the best or most appropriate explanation?

In addition, the peer students are interested in how the lessons are relevant for the summative assessment. For example, in the first case study, the peer teachers provided an overview of the most important topics in the syllabus. However, because the peer teachers have not yet finished the course, there will be less certainty regarding this issue. This stands in contrast to "cross-level" peer teaching which often will have a much stronger focus on the final exam. In modeling the problem-solving, these peer teachers can also tend to be more direct in the resolution of doubts (Duran & Topping, 2017).

Another important question is whether the same-level peer teacher can become too similar to the peer student regarding the level of background knowledge. If students are not challenged enough, there will be much less movements in the zone of cognitive proximity. In a worst-case scenario, is there a risk that poor peer teaching can have a potentially detrimental effect on the learning outcomes? Although there is an obvious risk of reducing the level of the academic learning, peer teachers still have the advantage in having recently acquired an understanding of the material. This can sometimes make them better in explaining issues regarding the subject matter because they are better in remembering the details of the learning process (Duran & Topping, 2017).

The zone of social proximity

Second, *the zone of social proximity* is orientated toward the student and addresses the group relationship between the students. Peer student learning can potentially contribute to a warmer and more informal atmosphere. One explanation is that the peer teachers and peer students share the same social background, including many of the same experiences, interests, and humor. This social proximity can potentially strengthen the spontaneous and informal aspects of the classroom interaction. Students will feel comfortable asking "silly" questions, honor misconceptions, and dare to be critical toward each other in a constructive way. Especially the second case study illustrates that students organized little whole-class discussions because they wanted to avoid critical or challenging questions. The class atmosphere was not always good and illustrates that differences in the peer teaching design will influence on the quality of the learning environment. With the zone of social proximity, it becomes important to ask how students and teachers ideally should communicate with each other.

Still, peer teachers will usually be more interested in the peer students as persons and show more empathy toward their learning situation. They can also include their own learning history in their teaching, explaining how one can cope with typical challenges and utilize different learning strategies. Because they are more familiar with the potential frustrations peer students are likely to face, they can provide better emotional support.

In combination, these particularities suggest that peer student learning represents a specific type of pedagogical practice. Some of its characteristics, such as proximity to the problem-solving process or the emphasis on personal student life stories, are very hard, if not impossible, for a formal teacher to include in the teaching. If this approach to teaching is to be valued, one needs to acknowledge that good teaching is not only about subject matter expertise, but also about getting students involved in the learning process.

7 Perspectives on collective peer learning

Introduction

The third main argument is that collective peer learning is one of three learning positions in collective peer teaching. On the one hand, this type of learning is closely linked to the instructional design since it focuses on how the whole group learn from each other through different kinds of organization. The qualitative systematic review displayed less data on collective peer learning position compared with the other two learning positions. The most obvious reason is the lack of qualitative studies that describe same-level collective peer teaching. However, both the case studies in this book provide more insight into how learning at a collective level between the students. In this section, collective peer learning will be further discussed in relation to what is labeled as whole-group structure, whole-group relations, whole-group knowledge, whole-group feedback, and whole-group diversity.

Whole-group structure

Switching positions

In collective peer teaching, all students at the "same level" are assigned to become peer teachers for each other over a short period of time. Depending on the design, they will either choose lesson content they have a special interest in, or they will be assigned by the teacher to learn a new topic before they teach it to others. The design principle resembles cooperative learning which also students become "experts" in an area before they share their knowledge with others (Johnson, 1994).

An interesting empirical finding is that some students comment that they learn about teaching by comparing their own lesson with others lessons they participate in. The rotation of roles, being both a peer teacher and a peer student, allows for a combination of self-observation and observation of other peer teachers. It was in the case study that some students highlighted the type of observational learning that builds on the switching of learning positions. In this collective peer teaching design, all students would both be peer teachers and peer students in many different classrooms over just two days.

None of the collective peer teaching studies in the review mention the learning benefits of switching between these two roles. One explanation may be that all the instructional designs organized the peer teaching over a longer period with weekly contributions (Aslan, 2015, 2017a, 2017b; Velez et al., 2011). However, this switching of roles has been identified in microteaching in teacher education. In a study by Ralph (2014), the second largest positive finding category was the benefit of receiving and giving peer feedback after the microteaching. This teaching is typically done in groups of only five to ten students, which creates a more comfortable feedback atmosphere. In the study, one student describes how one can observe other peers struggling with the same challenges: "I had the opportunity to watch others going through the same struggles as me. This allowed me to see in application why certain teaching strategies are more or less effective than others" (Ralph, 2014, p. 22). The quote illustrates how learning emerges through a combination of self-observation and observation of others, which allows for reflection on what teaching strategies are most effective. It appears that this proximity in time allows for a more "natural" comparison of the many different pedagogical practices, including your own. The drawback is that some are not able to pay attention properly to other lesson before they have finished their own. In the second case study, fewer students report of this problem with a likely reason being that the peer teaching was spread over weekly lessons.

Since all students got the same task, students could observe how other peers solved the teaching challenge in different ways. Especially in the second case study, peer teachers could also adjust their plans based on their observations of previous peer lessons. This type of peer modeling allows for what can be labeled as near-peer learning, modeling of pedagogical practices in a transparent learning environment (Lave & Wenger, 1991).

These processes resemble a professional learning, which create recurring cycles of action and reflection following the new peer lessons every week. The main difference is that students did not get the opportunity to improve their own lesson in a second round. Instead, the learning cycle was a collective level, with new peer teachers adjusting their lesson to what other peer teachers had previously done. A major disadvantage in both case studies was the lack of time dedicated to repeated reflective discussions around the lessons.

The main difference in "cross-level" peer teaching is that only one person or a few persons will serve as role models. They can have strong social and attitudinal effects because they model the behavior or preferred skill level that peer students are expected to reach after they have completed the course (Topping & Ehly, 1998).

Fair division of work

Fair teaching can be regarded as a core value in all teaching. In most types of group work, it will be a challenge to ensure that students perceive the collective work as fair in different ways (Baltzersen, 2017, pp. 293–299), also by avoiding free riders (Johnson & Johnson, 2018). This is usually less of a problem in collective peer teaching because everyone contributes with a lesson. For example, in the first case study, there were no complaints about free riders or unfairness. Since all peer teacher teams were given the same amount of lesson time, this was perceived as fair.

However, in the second case study, several students found the workload to be unfair. Because some of the lessons were organized differently, this increased the perception of unfairness. Consequently, some peer teacher groups got more and less work than others. It illustrates the importance of giving students approximately the same tasks. A few students also mentioned other issues such as unequal contributions within the peer teacher groups, and lessons being held at different times which gave some less time to write about this topic in the term paper. One student felt that the variations in peer lessons between the four classes were unfair. These comments illustrate why standardized teaching, delivering the same "package of content to everybody at the same time" is so prevalent. It ensures that students perceive the learning process and the exam preparations as fair.

Whole-group relations

With a few exceptions, students in both case studies report of a good atmosphere in the class. In the first case study, one student stated being in a "community of equals." The term "equals" does not only refer to a symmetrical group relationship, but it refers to a shared responsibility for the learning process. Students felt the importance of everybody contributing to the collective learning process. In the first case study, the rotation was done so frequently that all students were involved in peer teaching in just two days. The tight schedule with many short lessons appears to strengthen the feeling of belonging to a symmetrical community of learners.

According to Martin (2018), a unique characteristic of peer teaching is that the control of the lesson is transferred to the students. It suggests a change of roles in the classroom toward stronger empowerment and democratic participation in classroom learning. Every student will enter a role of temporary asymmetry present. A student entering the role of a teacher, the most powerful position in class, is expected to communicate with the rest of the group in this role. When a peer teacher engages the class in dialogues or different learning activities, this person is likely to become better acquainted with the rest of the group. The combination of student-active methods and shifts in being peer teachers, made it possible for many students to communicate with each other in new ways. During this process, it is likely that the students also get better acquainted with each other.

Some peer teaching studies also found that students are pleased to help others, achieving a sense of fulfillment or self-actualization. For instance, in the study by Lockspeiser et al. (2008), the peer teachers appreciated not only the opportunity to relearn the subject matter, but also to have contact with first-year students. In addition, the peer teachers were happy they could give something back to the medical school community. In microteaching too, a positive learning environment is important. In one study, a student underlines the importance of a supportive atmosphere: "There was a real sense of community in our class. This is the best example of learning from your peers, plus it was so much fun" (Ralph, 2014, p. 23). By being part of a trusting milieu, the student also felt more free to take risks (Ralph, 2014). According to Topping (2017, pp. 37, 40), an open and positive climate also makes it easier to experiment with new teaching methods that might fail.

Furthermore, the whole-group relations will be influenced by the teaching methods that are used, ranging from a minimum of contact in a monological lecture to a lesson that invites students to discuss issues. In general, peer teachers in both case studies were able to create a warmer class atmosphere based on more symmetrical group relations. However, in the second case study, some peer teachers in one of the classes (seminar groups) interacted very little with the student group. The students also reported that the class atmosphere was not optimal, but it is unclear why it became like this.[1]

In contrast, if there is a sense of communality, students will feel more comfortable to freely exchange ideas, which can lead to deeper levels of understanding (Velez et al., 2011). In cross-level peer teaching, the learning atmosphere will also usually be experienced as better, with peer students feeling more comfortable asking for help and being less stressed about the exam (Evans & Cuffe, 2009; Rees et al., 2016). One important reason is that peer teachers often show a more genuine interest in the students. They are more willing to engage in a closer and informal relationship with the peer students because they can more easily empathize with them compared with a faculty teacher (Lockspeiser et al., 2008; Loda et al., 2019).

Whole-group knowledge

Sharing of whole-group knowledge in a face-to-face setting

Can the whole class produce relevant knowledge? In the first case study, the peer teaching addressed the 42 topics that were relevant for oral exam the second final year. There were many different peer lessons during the two days of peer teaching, and students commented that it gave them a good overview of the most important topics in the course. They felt the lessons prepare them well for the final exam. Each topic had an independent value that the students required to have knowledge of. Here, there were no student comments that complained about the lack of coherence between the lessons.

In contrast, in the second case study, some students mentioned that peer teaching created fragmented learning and lack of deep learning across lessons. One explanation was that each lesson was reduced from 45 to 35 minutes. In addition, a two-hour lesson would be split into shorter lessons that might address quite different topics. In both case studies, there was little time dedicated to critical evaluation of the lesson content. The formal teachers seldom had time to provide more theoretical explanations or address any misconceptions in large detail. Often, both the peer and formal teacher feedback was also more directed toward the teaching performance than the subject matter itself.

If there had been more reflective discussions after the lessons, this could have stimulated deeper learning of the subject matter. One advantage with peer teaching, is that students usually are more critical toward the peer teacher explanations. This can trigger more disagreements which can develop the students' critical thinking and further elaboration around the issue. Misconceptions are not necessarily negative but can offer new opportunities for learning. For example, in science education today, there is less focus on extinguishing misconceptions, but rather to create awareness in students that their beliefs are not accurate from a scientific point of view (Vosniadou, 2020). Another example is the peer instruction method developed by Eric Mazur (1997). Here, misconceptions play an essential part in facilitating learning. Students in small-group assignments are challenged to convince each other by explaining the reasons behind their proposed solutions. To stimulate the best discussions, students are encouraged to find other students who disagree with their proposed answer. Peer explanations differ from the teacher's explanation because students are typically uncertain about whether the explanation is correct, whereas the teacher is always expected to communicate the correct answer (Crouch et al., 2007). Although the teacher's explanation is usually the most efficient route from question to answer, the students' explanations are often more convincing.

However, especially the second case study shows that students were reluctant to pose any critical questions even when not happy with the lesson. In the written peer feedback, they would also emphasize giving praise. This indicates that collective synthesizing efforts on the subject matter need to be an explicit part of the instructional design. If students are to compare and elaborate on the lesson content, this should be as a part of an assignment. One example could be to let students organize a peer review of the written summaries. This type of collective learning resembles a pedagogical approach like knowledge building. Here, the whole class will together actively monitor their collective understanding of the learning material and decide on how they can further develop it (Scardamalia & Bereiter, 2006). knowledge building emphasizes the collective production and advancement of community knowledge—that is, knowledge comparable to the "state of the art" in a discipline, profession, or industry. While brainstorming may be easy, sustained creative work with ideas is harder and often largely absent from the educational experience. In this pedagogy, priority is given to improving ideas, rather than simply sharing or evaluating ideas (Scardamalia & Bereiter, 2021).

Although there are examples of the whole class being able to have a meta-discourse about their collective work (Baltzersen, 2013b, 2013c), there is still need for support from a formal teacher. Furthermore, if students are allowed to choose their own topics on their own interest, the formal teacher will need to ensure that the lesson content is relevant for the learning objectives and the syllabus. Ideally, the peer teachers should receive some kind of feedback on their interpretation of the subject matter as a peer teacher. According to Martin (2018), the role of the formal teacher in collective peer teaching is to ensure that the students understand the given material, help them reduce complexity, and focus on the essential parts of the academic content (Martin, 2018). Ideally, collective peer teaching will bridge the student's perspective on the subject matter with the perspective of the formal teacher on the subject matter.

Sharing of whole-group knowledge in an online setting

Regarding whole-group knowledge, another interesting question is if the student group can produce something of value to others outside class? In collective peer teaching, the core activity centers on verbal sharing of knowledge in a physical face-to-face setting. In addition, the peer teachers shared their teaching material, especially their presentation slides in the online learning platform. In the second case study, a relatively large number of students tell that they had read and reused these resources when working with the term paper. In the first case study, the students also shared written summaries on the topic, which intended to provide a good overview of the most important topics in the syllabus. When all students examined a part of the syllabus in detail and shared this knowledge with the rest of the class, they were able to collectively prepare for the final exam. Some of the summaries where also edited by the formal teacher and shared openly with others outside of class. These articles were later reused by new students in the course and other outsiders.

Another option would have been to let new peer teachers build on the collective knowledge that previous students have produced. Knowledge sharing primarily happened in the class, but not to the same degree for all students across classes. Then it would need to be part of the design that new peer teachers are expected to build on and teach what previous students have focused on. Or this should perhaps the formal teacher do. For examples, wikis have been used in education to support this kind of collective knowledge advancement (Baltzersen, 2010, 2017).

Furthermore, in the first case study, a small group of students also made instructional videos as a part of an alternative assignment. The online videos comprised a collection that was shared between everyone in the course. Feedback was given as an asynchronous comment from peers and the teacher.

Because this was done in an online environment that everyone in the class had access to, all students could read and give comments. Still, the main limitation with instructional videos is that they are primarily build on monological "Knowledge telling." Discussions depend on student interest afterward and will emerge asynchronously over time. Although these videos were not shared openly on the internet, they helped strengthen a culture of sharing in the course in contrast to cultures that are dominated by individualized competition between students.

However, the instructional videos were notpublished. One primary concern is ensuring compliance with copyright rules when the student producers did not receive any individual guidance on their work. Additionally, the public benefits of open publishing greatly depends on the effort students invest in their work.

Whole-group feedback

In whole-group feedback, all students are involved in giving feedback in different ways. When variations in the quality of the peer teaching are to be expected, it becomes even more important to evaluate the teaching in a critical and systematic manner. The basic idea is that by scaling up the amount and diversity of the feedback, one can improve the learning process. The evaluation of collective peer teaching can be done at different levels. At a micro level, every lesson can be evaluated in relation to the teaching performance. At a macro level, the evaluation can be directed toward the complete instructional design and the learning outcomes.

If we look at both case studies, each lesson was evaluated separately. After the lesson, all students in class were invited to give brief verbal feedback or written feedback immediately in an online form. By using an online evaluation form, it was easy for all students to give feedback at the same time. All peer teachers in the first case study and a majority in the second, preferred to use "the two stars and a wish" rubric to receive peer feedback. It emphasizes positive comments and suggestions on improvement. Most of the written feedback was anonymous. In addition, the formal teacher also gave brief verbal feedback. A difference in the second case study was that the discussions with the teacher was longer because some of the time in the break was used too. This conversation would typically begin with the peer teachers first doing a self-evaluation. In other studies of collective peer teaching, the peer teachers will also receive feedback after the lesson, either by the formal teacher or by the student group (Velez et al., 2011).

The learning value of receiving peer feedback

When comparing the perceived learning value of peer feedback between two case studies, significant differences emerge. In the first study, most students appreciated the feedback, while a significant group in the second study found it less valuable. This is surprising as both studies employed similar feedback methods, including verbal comments after the lesson and opportunities to give written comments. A possible explanation might be that the second group lacked the skills to provide pertinent feedback. As Topping (2009) suggests, students need to learn how to offer constructive feedback. For example, in one study of microteaching, a student underscores the learning value of giving structured peer feedback, "We learned from our peers by watching their reactions, and by also having to evaluate them using the forms" (Ralph, 2014, p. 23). This quote suggests that observation forms can be useful in improving the quality of the peer feedback. For example, peer teachers could spend more time devising their feedback questions rather than resorting to simpler methods like "two star and a wish."

Another reason is that more students in the second case study were not motivated to put much effort into the feedback because it was anonymous and didn't count as a part of the final assessment. In general, this student group was also more dissatisfied with the whole collective peer teaching design. Many preferred using "minimum strategies" in their feedback.

The overall learning effect of peer feedback may be debatable, but its potential to boost student self-confidence is noteworthy. Studies show that peer teachers value praise from classmates (Velez et al., 2011). Despite peer feedback often being of lower quality than teacher feedback, its volume and immediacy may compensate for this deficiency. While teacher feedback is usually seen as authoritative, peer feedback often provides a richer dialogue, more open for negotiations (Topping, 2009).

By involving all students in giving separate feedback, different individuals can be attentive toward various aspects of the lesson. However, many provided only brief and general comments, reducing the learning value. Despite anonymity, students often hesitate to give constructive critique. To ensure helpful whole-group feedback, a minimum quality level is needed. Even when the primary aim is to support the peer teacher learning, the peer students will also learn by giving feedback. It may also sharpen their attentiveness, positively impacting the learning during the lesson (Black & Wiliam, 1998; Topping, 2009).

Furthermore, by involving everyone in giving and receiving more feedback, this empowers the student voice. If feedback is given verbally in class, all can learn from listening to others' comments. Subsequent discussions could stimulate critical thinking and should be integral to the collective peer teaching design.

One of the goals with whole-group feedback is to boost students' collaborative abilities in a professional learning community. However, opinions on public vs. private evaluations varied among the second case study's students. Many struggled to discuss teaching post-lesson, suggesting a lack of familiarity with open feedback cultures. This is paradoxical, as research emphasizes regular feedback for professional learning (Ericsson et al., 1993).

Despite this, many students in the first case study appreciated the brief peer feedback, suggesting that feeling of mastery after the lesson may suffice. Even demotivated students in the second case study reported a sense of accomplishment afterward. The general positive feedback could also have bolstered students' self-confidence.

Evaluation of the collective peer teaching design

Another type of whole-group feedback is characterized by letting all students evaluate the collective peer teaching design. In both case studies, this was done by responding to an online questionnaire at the end of the course. The student perceptions of their own learning provide important feedback to the formal teachers in their further improvement of the instructional design. In the questionnaire, the students were also asked about the relevance of collective peer teaching as a teaching method for their future work in schools. Especially, in the first case study most students found it to be highly relevant, indicating that this teaching method might be more relevant in upper secondary school than primary school.

Moreover, in the second case study, the formal teachers received constructive critique from student representatives during the course. For example, students addressed the need for better integration between the peer teaching, the faculty-led lectures. The two additional written assignments also gave information about how the students experienced the peer teaching. In the term paper, it was mandatory to write about peer teaching as a pedagogical practice. This allowed both for critical thinking around the learning process and valuable feedback to the course instructor.

Whole-group diversity

Does a collective peer teaching design utilize more diversity in the student group compared with other instructional designs? In comparing the two case studies, it is possible to identify several different whole-group diversity effects. First, the number of teachers increases, which leads to more variation in teaching styles, both presentation techniques and teaching methods. If students are allowed to specialize in different areas, this lesson content diversity will increase. Not least, when all students become peer teachers, there will be more differences in the quality of the teaching. In the empirical findings, several students highlight these different types of diversity as beneficial for their learning. In this section, they will be further analyzed and discussed.

Increasing the number of lessons

One of the most prominent characteristics with collective peer teaching is the radical increase in the number of teachers. In the first case study, the large group of students were divided into two classes which followed separate tracks. Twenty-eight lessons were organized over two days with each lesson lasting 25 minutes. Because of the short lessons, the teaching covered a more diverse set of topics than what was normal. In the second case study, a normal lesson of two hours was split into two shorter lessons which lasted around 35 minutes. Two different peer teacher groups would usually be responsible for each lesson. The lesson time was reduced by 10 minutes to allow for feedback from peers and teachers. On several occasions, the two peer teacher teams chose to collaborate to offer a more coherent lesson content. The feedback session would then only be after the second lesson.

In both case studies, there was frequent rotation of peer teachers in the lessons too, with several peer teachers switching on standing in front of the class. During one day of teaching in the first case study, 15–20 peer teachers would switch on being responsible for seven short lessons. In comparison, a faculty teacher would normally use one day to cover one or two topics with the whole student group.

One advantage with increasing the number of lessons is more variation in the teaching. When seven different peer teacher teams are responsible for one day of teaching, there is a much larger diversity of teaching styles at play. Especially in the first case study, this diversity increased both peer student engagement and motivation. In addition, the students enjoyed the time efficiency of the lessons and how they together summarized the first year of the course in a relevant way. In the second case study, the rotation of peer teachers was spread out throughout the semester and the perceived variation was not equally present.

Increasing the diversity of teaching styles

An unavoidable consequence of collective peer teaching is increased diversity of teaching styles, including both presentation techniques and active learning methods. The scaling of teachers also allows for many more personalities to lead classroom activities, which contributes to the perception of a more varied teaching in a positive manner. In the first case study, one student claimed it was easier to pay attention because of all the variations in lesson content and teaching methods. Most students became more engaged and less bored. The potential disadvantage fragmentation and lack of coherence between the lessons. If the learning periods become too short, this may also inhibit deep learning. For example, in the second case study several students commented that the 35-minute lessons were too short to allow for in-depth discussions. In addition, the removal of most of the faculty lectures gave fewer opportunities to follow up on the discussions later.

On the positive side, the frequent rotation of peer teachers sharpened the observational attention toward different teaching styles. In the first case study, several students highlight the opportunity to observe diverse teaching as the most positive factor in collective peer teaching. The proximity in time between the peer lessons spurred an interest in comparing the lesson, making it possible to be more attentive to detailed differences in the teaching. Because these peer teacher groups did their lesson preparations independent of each other, it is likely that this increased the diversity of teaching methods. Several students also underline the value of observing one's own teaching with others teaching. In the second case study, quite a large group of students report that they learned by observing fellow students teaching.

Likewise, in the review, Lockspeiser et al. (2008) find that students observe peer teachers with great interest. The peer students often identify themselves more strongly with their peer teachers. One explanation is that these peer teachers manifest the visible knowledge level which the peer students are close to reaching. In the teacher education context, especially studies of microteaching have found that student teachers value this type of observational learning. For instance, in one study, a student says, "It was good to watch others and learn from their teaching (…)" (Ralph, 2014, p. 23). While these studies have often focused on training of simple teaching skills, collective peer teaching addresses teaching proficiency in a broader sense. For instance, in the first case study, many students claim the observational learning strengthened their ability to think in new ways. The comments indicate that it was more to get new ideas or inspiration than solely imitating the peer teacher's demonstrations, which is more common in medical school (Rees et al., 2016).

When students are exposed to various teaching styles, the process becomes something else than observing a single "expert model teacher." Instead, the peer teachers model how teaching methods can be used in various ways. Especially the first case study show that students learned by observing a wide range of other teaching methods, even when the teaching was only briefly discussed with others in the class. In the teaching profession, observational learning (e.g. lesson study) is increasingly considered to be an important part of what characterizes professional learning communities (Baricaua Gutierez, 2016). Although this training of teaching skills at campus is not new, this model learning has usually been done as microteaching in small groups, with an emphasis on practicing specific skills.

In the second case study, the four peer teacher groups were more influenced by each other because they had a pre-mentoring session together. In addition, new peer teacher groups would learn from observing previous peer teaching lessons. It is likely that this resulted in lessons becoming more similar concerning the use of teaching methods. Still, the main advantage was that the formal teacher could raise critical questions regarding the teaching, for example, that many of the whole-class discussions were dominated by IRE communication (Cazden, 2001).

Increasing the lesson content diversity

In the case studies, there were significant differences regarding whether peer teachers could choose their lesson content based on their interests. In the second case study, the formal teachers had pre-selected the lesson content each weak. In the pre-mentoring session, they would have a short introductory lecture about the subject matter with academic recommendations. The disadvantage with this approach is that the students will teach topics they are less interested in. There is a risk that it may have a negative influence on the quality of the lesson, which this case study indicates. If most of the lessons are of low quality, this might even have a negative influence on the general learning outcome for all students.

In contrast, all peer teacher groups in the first case study could choose freely between as many as 42 academic topics. This increased the likelihood of finding a topic that matched their interests. Because of the large number of topics available, all the lessons were different from each other. Most of the students experienced the academic learning to be very good level. Findings from the first case study suggest that it is very important to give students enough time to prepare their lesson. The emphasis on academic quality was further strengthened by tasking students to write a summary of the academic topic. This text had to be above a certain minimum level of quality to be approved by the formal teacher. Furthermore, the quality of the lesson content in peer teaching will also depend on other factors such as the level of previous background knowledge and the degree of guidance from the formal teacher.

Here, there may be a potential conflict between individual learning preferences and the need for peer teaching of high quality. For instance, should you teach the topics where you already have the most background knowledge of should you choose an area where you lack background knowledge, but think you will learn more in the lesson preparations. Is the goal to maximize the individual learning or the academic quality of the peer lessons? This dilemma is present in other active learning methods like whole-class projects. In one study, the students divided the tasks according to their individual abilities, but afterward they suggested that they should instead had divided the tasks according to their learning needs. This could have strengthened the individual learning, but it would likely have reduced the overall quality of the collective work (Baltzersen, 2017, pp. 278–282).

Increasing the diversity of the quality of teaching

Another important characteristic with collective peer teaching is that the quality of the lessons will vary more compared with letting a few faculty teachers be responsible for most of the course. When all students in class are invited to become peer teachers, some differences in quality are inevitable.

For example, in the first case study, one-third had no previous teaching experience, while two-thirds had one year or more of experience. Therefore, some students had more self-confidence and a larger repertoire of teaching methods than others.

Regarding observational learning, it is interesting that students in both case studies claim they learned by observing variations in the quality of the teaching. It appears that a lack of quality or a "failed" lesson can be valuable in several different ways. Some student comments suggest that the reason is that poor teaching can, paradoxically, disclose mechanisms that are essential in good teaching. It is the "failure" that triggers the motivation to reflect around differences in teaching of high and low quality. The attentiveness toward variations in quality may have been reinforced because the peer teacher is a student, who is not yet fully qualified.

Although the peer teacher separately may be less capable of presenting the subject matter of an equally high quality as a professional teacher, they offer something extra at an aggregated level, more variation in teaching style and teaching method, and even lesson content. It creates a paradox in this type of teaching because it is less about the actual performance, but more about the reflection it triggers. However, one can question whether there should be a lower threshold for the quality of the lesson content in peer teaching. In the second case study, many students felt that too many lessons were of too low academic quality. If the quality in general is low, this will also result in less diversity in the quality of the peer teaching.

In campus-teaching in teacher education, learning by observing variations in quality is usually associated with microteaching. For example, in one microteaching study, a student mentions the value of observing what doesn't work: "I liked being able to watch my friends teach and then learn something from their successes (and failures), maybe noting things for yourself if you hadn't thought of them before" (Ralph, 2014, p. 22). If there is value in learning from failures, all types of teaching can be valuable. The comparison may even help identify the mechanisms that are crucial in successful teaching.

Concerning potential disadvantages, one can question if it is enough with tacit reflection through observation or if explicit feedback and discussions are required. In professional learning, feedback is considered an essential part of further improvement (Ericsson et al., 1993). This includes the ability to learn from your own mistakes and others (Argyris, 1991; Dreyfus & Dreyfus, 2005). This is especially relevant in teacher education which aims to strengthen prospective teachers in becoming reflective practitioners (Schön, 1984). If failure becomes acceptable, it may also be easier for the peer teachers to dare experiment with new teaching methods, thus strengthening their innovation competence. However, we do not know enough about the potential negative effects of performance anxiety related to peer lessons. Especially in second case study, quite a lot of students were very anxious or stressed about their own lesson. Likewise, a handful of students from the first case study struggled to concentrate on their peers' teaching, as nervousness regarding their impending lesson preoccupied them.

Summary—collective peer learning as collective intelligence

In this summary, research on collective intelligence (CI) is used as a theoretical framework to better explain the basic characteristics in collective peer learning position. Several other theoretical perspectives could have been relevant to include such as situated learning (Lave & Wenger, 1991), knowledge building (Scardamalia & Bereiter, 2006), critical pedagogy (Freire, 2005), and expansive learning (Engeström, 2014), but all of them appear somewhat limited in grasping the full complexity of collective learning processes. In educational research, CI has been used very little as a term. Inspired by Baltzersen (2022), collective peer learning is here connected to the following five CI principles: (1) Rotation (Whole-group structure), (2) Community of student experts (Whole-group relations), (3) Collective knowledge advancement (Whole-group knowledge), (4) Collective peer evaluation (Whole-group feedback), and (5) The wisdom of the student crowd (Whole-group diversity).

Rotation

In (CI) studies, 'rotation' is frequently spotlighted as a vital organizing principle. This term, in the context of group dynamics, refers to the periodic change or alternation of roles, participants, or perspectives to ensure a wider and more diverse engagement in various types of collective problem-solving. Notably, it enables the harnessing of diverse citizen expertise. For example, in the Citizen's Assembly in Ireland, rotation played a crucial role in ensuring fair and diverse discussions. This assembly is a group of randomly selected individuals, representing a diverse cross-section of the population, who come together to deliberate and make recommendations on specific political issues. Participants engaged in monthly small group conversations, with frequent rotations enhancing exposure to varied perspectives, thereby facilitating attitudinal change (Baltzersen, 2022, p. 358). Similarly, the Citizen's Assembly in Ostbelgian used a rotation system to broaden public participation in democratic decision-making by involving a large percentage of the population over time. Citizens fulfill their civic duty by participating intensely for a short period, knowing that fellow citizens will make similar contributions at another point of time. This modern democratic system draws inspiration from ancient Athens, where rotation and random sampling were key components of the first democracy (Baltzersen, 2022, p. 282). Rotation also ensures equitable contributions and fair work division in rule-governed collaborative problem-solving (Baltzersen, 2022, pp. 271–275).

Similarly, in collective peer teaching, lessons are organized according to different types of rotation. In a *parallel instructional design*, like in the first case study, all students rotate on being peer teachers within a short period of time. In contrast, a *sequentialized instructional design*, as seen in the second case study, spreads the rotation is spread over a more extended period, typically most of the course period. In peer teacher groups, the group members will often also rotate on standing in front of the class. Furthermore, the rotation of being both a peer teacher and a peer student, encourages self-observation and comparison with other peer teachers. Especially in the parallel instructional design the proximity in time between the different lessons will motivate this type of observational learning.

As a design method, rotation illustrates how knowledge sharing between students can be a formalized part of the teaching. The quality emerges through an exposure to a wide diversity of teaching strategies. Everyone makes a different contribution, but it is still similar in size, being responsible for one lesson each. When all students become peer teachers, they also participate on equal terms in the lesson. In the first case study, this frequent rotation of peer teaching created a strong sense of shared responsibility. However, in the second case study, students perceived the task sizes as unequal, leading to a perceived unfair workload.

Community of student experts

In CI research, rotation has been identified as a key element that promotes group cohesion. For instance, in certain animal groups on the move, there is a rotation of leadership roles. This practice seems to decrease the chances of the group breaking apart (Baltzersen, 2022, p. 107). The ancient Athenian democracy also utilized rotation methods, minimizing faction dominance by spreading responsibility across the Council. For example, each tribal team of 50 members led the Council for a tenth of the year, with a monthly lottery determining which tribe would hold the presidency. Daily, a new member was chosen by lot to serve as Athens' chief executive officer or president. This position could only be held once in a lifetime, resulting in a majority of Council members holding this important role during the year. This rotational system enhanced political participation and competence among Athenians (Baltzersen, 2022, p. 148).

Similarly, collective peer teaching thrives on rotational reorganization of group dynamics. By assuming the peer teacher role, students briefly experience asymmetrical relationships within the group. This dynamic ensures that each student engages in both symmetrical and asymmetrical relationships during the course. This reciprocal responsibility fosters a unique learning community where students serve as mutual helpers (Wenger, 1999).

Moreover, students engage in diverse relations with each other, not based on social preferences, but rather on what kind of expertise or background knowledge different individuals possess. When all students examine different aspects of the subject matter, it cultivates a community of expertise. Unlike situated learning, where near-peer help is informal and potentially one-sided (Lave & Wenger, 1991), collective peer teaching allows everyone to become near-peers, offering help in specific areas for a set period. However, the extent to which this promotes mutual aid outside of lessons remains unclear, although some studies suggest that an increased number of peer teachers can enhance the learning environment, like in the anatomy laboratory (Evans & Cuffe, 2009).

This model of everyone contributing and assisting each other opens the door for democratizing the knowledge production process. With students taking turns leading the class, their involvement is significantly amplified. As Paulo Freire suggested, emancipatory pedagogy necessitates a classroom role reversal, transforming students into teachers:

> Through dialogue, the teacher-of-the-students and the students-of-the-teacher cease to exist and a new term emerges: teacher-student with students-teachers. The teacher is no longer merely the-one-who-teaches, but one who is himself taught in dialogue with the students, who in turn while being taught also teach. They become jointly responsible for a process in which all grow.
>
> (Freire, 2005, p. 80)

This approach redistributes responsibility for learning and teaching, altering the power dynamics between students and the formal teacher and creating a more symmetrical group relationship. Both case studies indicate that collective peer teaching can enhance the class atmosphere by providing a more informal learning environment. However, the second case study highlights a reluctance among students to ask critical questions to each other, perhaps due to a lack of emphasis on peer critique in the broader teacher education program. It suggests that students may still perceive critique as the domain of the formal teacher.

Collective knowledge advancement

From a CI perspective, citizens offer unique insights into collective problem-solving that differ from formal experts or politicians. The advent of Web 2.0 has democratized knowledge production by facilitating open online knowledge sharing, permitting anyone to access, create, and disseminate knowledge (Baltzersen, 2022, pp. 50–75).

This raises the question: can students collectively generate valuable knowledge? It's crucial to consider whether the student's perspective on a subject matter holds intrinsic value, distinct from the formal teacher's viewpoint. Freire (2005) contends that it should be transformative, enabling individuals to critically understand their circumstances and societal power dynamics. This process involves exploring generative themes—central ideas derived from lived experiences, particularly of the oppressed. Such themes, rooted in learners' socio-political and cultural contexts, stimulate personal and societal transformation.

In a teacher education context, knowledge sharing can model a way of building professional knowledge. Students typically start a course with similar knowledge levels, but through lesson preparation, they gain specialized knowledge in various areas. In some courses, peer teachers could design lessons based on their personal experiences and narrative knowledge (Bruner, 1991), enhancing the richness and authenticity of learning.

Aggregating the lesson contributions

In collective peer teaching, the whole-group knowledge will consist of the aggregation of lesson contributions. The quality hinges on students' ability to leverage their background knowledge, interests, skills, and experiences. In the first case study, ample preparation time ensured students could advance their subject matter understanding. Since these students had also been part of the program for one year, many already acquired substantial knowledge about the lesson topics. Still, individual lesson contributions risked varying in quality.

In both case studies, students shared their presentation slides on an online learning platform. In the first case, students also exchanged written topic summaries, fostering a culture of knowledge sharing. This sharing, however, was confined to a restricted platform, with only select high-quality summaries being published in an open textbook after teacher editing.

In an educational setting, open online knowledge sharing can include a wide range of educational resources like open textbooks (Baltzersen, 2022, pp. 54–56) and instructional videos (Baltzersen, 2022, pp. 62–66). While some student-produced resources may hold limited value for outsiders, there are numerous instances of student work benefiting broader audiences, with instructional videos potentially having extensive reach.

Building on the lesson contributions

An important part of collective knowledge advancement is related to how digital information enables easy modification and improvement of existing knowledge. Wikipedia exemplifies this through its collective production, allowing anyone to refine others' work (Baltzersen, 2022, pp. 56–58). Nonetheless, collective peer teaching often falls short in synthesizing contributions across lessons. The primary academic challenge lies in discerning the interconnections between separate knowledge units in this design typically focused on equal individual contributions.

More time could be allotted for students to synthesize different academic topics in the lessons, potentially with guidance from the formal teacher. Pedagogies like knowledge building enable the whole class to collaboratively develop and evaluate ideas (Scardamalia & Bereiter, 2006).

Such an approach necessitates the formal teacher organizing reflective communication or metadiscourses at various points (Baltzersen, 2013a, 2013c), akin to the organization of scientific expertise into complex knowledge bundles, not just separate units (Sawyer, 2022). Another possibility could involve successive student groups continue to build on the work of previous student groups, both by adding new contributions and modify existing ones. In an educational setting, there are also examples of students publishing articles in global online communities like Wikipedia (Baltzersen, 2017) and other wiki sites like Wikibooks (Baltzersen, 2010). This design allows synthesizing efforts to form part of an evolving collective work.

Collective peer evaluation

In the age of digitalization, reputation society has emerged, with ratings, reviews, and recommendations significantly influencing decisions and social dynamics. Online platforms and social media play a crucial role in this context, shaping reputations that affect success, credibility, and social standing (Baltzersen, 2022, pp. 341–349).

Collective peer teaching aligns with this trend, increasing feedback loops and the number of individuals providing feedback. Despite time constraints during verbal feedback sessions, digital feedback allowed all students to participate. Furthermore, students were invited to evaluate the entire instructional design.

Interest in collective peer evaluations has grown, driven by educational research highlighting the learning benefits of both giving and receiving peer feedback (Black & Wiliam, 1998; Topping, 2009) and the ease of organizing feedback via digital tools. Another explanation is how digital peer assessment tools have made it easy to organize many students in giving each other feedback. For example, it has become much simpler to let several persons comment on the same individual work. When the quality of the peer feedback varies a lot, scaling of the feedback increases the likelihood of receiving high-quality feedback. Still, the second case study shows that if students lack sufficient background knowledge or motivation, the quality of feedback may suffer, despite its scale.

In large courses, the volume of feedback can become overwhelming. Effective peer evaluations should involve reflective communication (Argyris & Schön, 1997; Baltzersen, 2022, pp. 349–355), not just information generation. While course instructors can interpret feedback privately, inviting students to discuss feedback can enhance understanding of the subject matter, specific lessons, or the overall instructional design. Thus, systematic student feedback can drive continuous improvement of instructional design through learning cycles.

The wisdom of the student crowd

The wisdom of the crowd refers to the phenomenon where the collective judgment, opinion, or estimation of a diverse group of people tends to be more accurate or insightful than that of an individual or a small group of experts. This requires four conditions. First, the group should be diverse, so different individuals can supplement each other with different pieces of information. Second, the group needs to be decentralized, without anyone directing the answers from the center. Third, individual opinions need to be aggregated into a collective opinion. Aggregation typically depends on numerical contributions and statistical methods. Fourth, the individuals in the crowd should act independently of each other. By pooling the knowledge and perspectives of a large number of people, this can lead to better decision-making, problem-solving, and forecasting (Baltzersen, 2022, pp. 10–11; Surowiecki, 2005).

This raises the question: Can a student group exhibit this wisdom? In the first case study, students favored peer teaching over faculty teaching. The second case study yielded mixed opinions, but the favorable findings prompted further investigation into collective peer teaching as a potential alternative to traditional faculty teaching. The argument hinges on the notion that the class's collective diversity can surpass the quality of instruction delivered by a single teacher. The case studies reveal several diversity types, such as lesson numbers, teaching styles, content, and teaching quality.

To better understand this diversity, we can distinguish between "learning-in-diversity" and "learning-from-diversity." The former refers to the inherent exposure to diversity within the instructional design, related to the pedagogical principle of variation. The latter pertains to the active reflection associated with different types of observational learning. Table 7.1 provides an overview.

Learning-in-diversity

Variation is integral to collective peer teaching, serving to enhance student engagement and reduce boredom. This diversity is introduced by each student's unique teaching style, methods, and lesson content, although the latter must remain within a range ensuring relevance to the learning process.

If students are allowed to choose topics freely, they may emphasize some areas more than others. Often, the formal teacher will need to help connect the separate lessons and address "missing" topics. For example, in the second case study, some students felt that the faculty teacher did not fulfill this purpose. A significant design challenge lies in balancing student and formal teacher contributions.

On the one hand, granting students full autonomy to teach their preferred topics can bolster independent lesson contributions. A classical wisdom of crowd perspective (Surowiecki, 2005) suggests this approach enhances the aggregated quality of the lessons. In this educational context, a *parallel*

Table 7.1 The characteristics of learning-in-diversity vs learning-from-diversity: an overview

1. Learning-in-diversity" (The variation bonus)	2. Learning-from-diversity" (Observational learning)
- Diversity which is inherent in the instructional design by increasing (scaling) the number of lessons and (peer) teachers. - Indirect exposure to diversity. Involves all students as they move through the different lesson contributions. - Variation as a pedagogical principle. More student engagement because of variation: - Lesson diversity refers to diversity of teaching styles, teaching methods, lesson content, and quality of the teaching. - Balancing student contributions versus formal teacher contributions - Independent lessons increase diversity (Parallel collective peer teaching) versus dependent lessons which reduce diversity (Sequentialized collective peer teaching).	- Diversity related to active individual reflection. - Because it requires conscious awareness of the diversity, there will be individual differences in the perceived presence of this diversity. - Observational learning is key pedagogical principle: Active comparison of different aspects of the lessons, comparison of others teaching, comparison of one's own teaching with others teaching, and the quality of the teaching. - Can include explicit discussions, but this is not necessary.

collective peer teaching design is optimal because it let peer teacher groups prepare their lessons at approximately the same time. This makes students less likely to copy each other in the selection of teaching methods. The downside is potential irrelevance to course objectives and challenges in synthesizing the lesson content.

One solution, as seen in the first case study, involved offering a choice of forty-two course-relevant topics, thereby mapping the entire subject area collectively—an approach akin to environmental sensing (Baltzersen, 2022, pp. 114–124). This strategy simultaneously amplified student motivation and satisfaction with academic learning.

On the other hand, having the formal teacher preselect lesson content can guarantee covering essential material, as in the second case study where teacher educators introduced key content in pre-mentoring sessions. This approach, however, may underutilize group diversity and depend heavily on formal teacher input. Despite this, the pedagogical practice still deviated from standardized teaching as peer lessons remained distinct, with peer teacher groups granted autonomy to interpret academic topics. A key design question is what the acceptable degree of student perspective on subject matter can be. Peer teaching may be less relevant in highly syllabus-centered courses where formal teachers can better communicate the content.

Perspectives on collective peer learning 113

In a *sequentialized collective peer teaching design* like in the second case study, the first peer teacher groups will also establish norms regarding what kind of teaching is acceptable. Here, students will be more influenced by each other through observational learning. This could be both beneficial, sparking ideas for students' lessons, and detrimental, risking replication of suboptimal instructional methods such as IRE communication (Cazden, 2001).

The importance of connecting and synthesizing different lesson contributions is another design consideration. If no "canonical" academic content exists and varied lesson content is valuable, collective peer teaching emerges as a fitting approach. It unveils multiple paths to deep learning and welcomes unexpected insights. However, excessive diversity can lead to confusion and fragmented learning. Conversely, if there's only one correct syllabus interpretation, inviting diverse student contributions becomes less relevant.

Learning-from-diversity

The diversity inherent in collective peer teaching fosters interest and enables comparison of varied teaching approaches. This comparison serves three key purposes. First, it allows students to assess different teaching styles and methods, inspiring them to adapt their own practice. In teacher education, exposure to a range of teaching techniques is crucial in nurturing reflective practitioners and developing unique professional teaching styles. Second, it facilitates a metacognitive interplay between self-observation and observing others' lessons, as students alternate between peer teacher and peer student roles. Lastly, it allows students to discern disparities in teaching quality, fostering critical thinking about the aggregate learning benefits derived from diverse lessons. Even less successful lessons can stimulate reflection on effective teaching and underscore the importance of learning from failure, laying the groundwork for improvement (Argyris, 1991; Dreyfus & Dreyfus, 2005).

In learning-from-diversity, collective peer teaching therefore amplifies opportunities for observation, comparison, and reflection, enhancing both model learning and critical thinking. However, as suggested by the second case study, a formal teacher's presence is necessary to prompt deeper critique, such as the lack of dialogical teaching and prevalence of IRE communication in many lessons (Cazden, 2001).

Collective peer teaching as human swarm problem-solving

Collective peer teaching is likened to "human swarm problem solving" as defined in CI research (Baltzersen, 2022, pp. 124–135). *First*, it engages with predefined problems - all students aim to solve a similar problem, doing a good lesson within the same time constraint (e.g., 25 minutes). *Second*, the problem-solving procedures are partially predetermined, with peer teachers required to engage students through active learning methods. *Third*, the problem-solving process is time-bound, with students given a specific period for preparation and execution. In the second case study, students were only given a week to prepare. While students were given more time to prepare in the first case study, the actual teaching performance was conducted over just two days.

Fourth, the collective peer teaching facilitated individual learning. In swarm problem-solving, there will also be a tradeoff between letting the individuals make independent contributions versus letting the individuals learn from each other. In the original wisdom of crowd approach (Surowiecki, 2005), the ideal is to avoid learning to reduce negative social influence such as herding effects (Baltzersen, 2022, p. 132). On the one hand, if we look at the parallel collective peer teaching design in the first case study, the lessons were made largely independently, fostering diversity of thinking in the lesson preparations. Since all students were given the same assignment, this spurred an interest in observing and comparing how others solve the "same problem" of designing a good lesson. This transparent learning environment allows for equal contribution, and learning is triggered by observing diverse lessons in close succession.

Conversely, the sequentialized design in the second case study provided much more opportunities for peer teacher groups to learn from each other over time, both in the pre-mentoring sessions and through observing previous lessons. This likely reduced lesson diversity in terms of teaching methods and organization.

Note

1 See the Appendix, *Table 9.16* Perceived learning outcome of peer teaching split on the four different seminar groups.

8 Conclusion—final remarks

The interplay between the three learning positions

Peer teaching studies typically affirm their value as supplements to faculty instruction and traditional lectures (Rees et al., 2016). Yet, our understanding of the impact of students replacing a formal teacher for an extended period in a collective peer teaching design remains limited. The field of learning-by-teaching is often skewed toward empirical findings, with theoretical discussions about the learning process being overlooked. This book contributes primarily by introducing a theoretical framework that facilitates a systematic exploration of the diverse learning processes emerging through collective peer teaching.

The systematic qualitative review, case studies analysis, and theoretical dissection presented here delve into the characteristics of three learning positions, each associated with different learning theories. In *peer teacher learning*, the essence lies in deep learning, propelled by the sense of social responsibility students feel toward their peers. This requires a delicate balance of social motivation and performance anxiety.

Peer student learning, inspired by Vygotsky, focuses on the unique aspect of peer teaching that derives from increased proximity. This book distinguishes between the spheres of social and cognitive proximity. Social proximity emphasizes close group relationships, while cognitive proximity pertains to a student-oriented perspective on the subject matter, aligning with students' learning needs and incorporating practical experience.

Collective peer learning accentuates learning through exposure to diversity, inspired by the concept of collective intelligence. This emerges through varied lessons, collective peer evaluations, collective knowledge advancement, and the development of a community of student experts. This is possible because peers have different levels of expertise, knowledge, or experience which they share in a transparent learning environment. Through observational learning, the students learn by comparing their own contributions with other peers' work. Enhancing this learning level necessitates reflective communication to synthesize student-generated knowledge.

DOI: 10.4324/9781003403586-8
This chapter has been made available under a CC-BY-NC-ND 4.0 license.

116 Conclusion—final remarks

The central argument posits that a single learning theory cannot fully encapsulate the complexity of the learning process. It advocates examining how these three learning positions—peer teacher learning, peer student, and collective peer learning—coexist and operate concurrently. This book's empirical findings substantiate that each learning position possesses unique learning mechanisms.

Table 8.1 exemplifies how the three different learning positions can interact at the same time in collective peer teaching.

Table 8.1 An overview of the interplay between the three different learning positions

Learning activity	Peer teacher learning position	Peer student learning position	Collective learning position
Explanation	- Learning by preparing an explanation - Learning by presenting a relevant explanation - Learning by answering a question or asking a question	- Learning by receiving an explanation - Learning by asking a question - Learning by receiving a more relevant explanation	- Learning by comparing peer teacher explanations with explanation provided by the formal teacher or the textbook explanation
Misconceptions	- Learning by receiving critique of the concepts or explanations in the presentation	- Learning by being critical toward the content in the lesson and possible misconceptions	- Learning by comparing variations in the quality of the lessons, both regarding subject matter and teaching methods
Student expertise	- Learning through extensive and repeated work on the subject matter. Planning the lesson, conducting the lesson and evaluating the lesson. Work in several phases and cycles	- Learning from the peer teacher who has specialized within one topic and developed more expertise than other students, but still familiar with students' learning needs	- Learning by getting an overview of the most important topics through many different lessons ("Teaching to the test") - Learning by observing and comparing different teaching methods
Engagement	- Learning by providing engaging teaching. Transformation of abstract subject matter into engage didactical content	- Learning through active participation (e.g. having fun—not being bored)	- More engagement because of more variation in teaching methods and different teaching styles

(Continued)

Table 8.1 (Continued)

Learning activity	Peer teacher learning position	Peer student learning position	Collective learning position
Peer feedback	- Learning by receiving peer feedback on the peer teaching. Both verbal and in written anonymous form. Receiving richer and more diverse peer feedback	- Learning by giving peer feedback on the peer teaching - Learning how to give feedback	- Learning by being part of more open feedback processes and reflective discussions
Emotional support	- Learning by giving emotional support to student challenges	- Learning by receiving emotional support to student challenges	- Improving the class atmosphere, the relations, and communication between the students in class
Social competence	- Learning to be responsible for others learning	- Learning to respect the peer teacher position	- Learning about the benefits of being part of collective learning processes

The table illustrates that several types of learning will occur at the same time in the classroom.

Rather than focusing solely on peer student learning, it may be pertinent to address all three types of learning—the peer teacher, peer student, and collective peer learning. Notably, collective peer learning emerges more prominently in the context of collective peer teaching.

Theoretically, these three learning positions can be seen as components of a "germ cell" (Baltzersen, 2017, pp. 58–64), constituting the foundational elements of classroom learning. They function according to a dialectical logic. For example, peer teacher learning occurs when the peer teacher gives an explanation. At the same time the peer students will learn something from this explanation. Additionally, the peer student can compare this explanation to those from formal teachers, textbooks, or other peers, fostering academic learning in the interplay between peer and faculty teaching.

This dialectical interplay manifests in various ways. In collective peer teaching, peer teacher learning delves into in-depth comprehension, while peer student learning strives for a broad overview of course topics. Student motivation derives from both the role of a peer teacher and participation in others' lessons. Students, in learning teaching skills, tend to contrast their lessons with their peers'. If teaching is assumed to be multifaceted with no single best approach, exposure to diverse teaching styles becomes valuable. Developing teaching proficiency necessitates reflective engagement on what works and what doesn't.

The outlined learning positions could guide further research into collective peer teaching as a distinct pedagogical practice. Intriguing questions arise: is this theoretical framework applicable to other pedagogical practices? Does collective peer teaching expand our comprehension of classroom learning? Are there always three distinct learning positions in a classroom? Are processes of collective peer learning present even in traditional, transmission-oriented teaching?

Transforming campus into practice—implications for teacher education

Within teacher education, collective peer teaching has the potential to bridge the gap between theoretical knowledge and actual practice (Darling-Hammond, 2006). This approach offers students a platform to mature as reflective practitioners (Schön, 1984); aligning their pedagogical beliefs (espoused theories) with their pedagogical actions (theories-in-use) (Argyris & Schon, 1992). Moreover, this approach to teaching cultivates a stronger professional learning community where all students actively support each other, through shared lessons and peer feedback.

Viewed narrowly, this form of peer teaching can be regarded as an advanced variation of microteaching. In a wider lens, it signifies an innovative strategy to empower student teachers. Considering the global emphasis on 21st-century skills like creativity, collaboration, and critical thinking, collective peer teaching emerges as a compelling pedagogical alternative.

Despite its promise, its presence is scarce in teacher education. The landscape remains dominated by traditional lectures and exams, leaving considerable room for communities of student expertise to take center stage in learning.

Nonetheless, this book seeks to catalyze the shift. It presents a theoretical framework and compelling arguments for the efficacy of collective peer teaching to enhance student learning. Hopefully, future research will delve deeper, exploring the optimization of diverse collective peer teaching designs and further discuss the role of the teacher educator—a topic lightly touched upon herein.

Appendix

First case study

Table A.1 Comparison of the perceived quality of the peer teaching with the faculty-led traditional lectures during the first year of the teacher education program

(N = 58)	Percentage frequency distribution (%)
Significantly worse than a traditional lecture	2
Somewhat worse than a traditional lecture	12
Approximately as good as a traditional lecture	38
Somewhat better than a traditional lecture	35
Significantly better than a traditional lecture	14

Table A.2 Student perceptions of learning by teaching (percentage frequency distribution)

(N = 58)	1: Not satisfied	2	3	4	5: Very satisfied	Mean	National mean[1]
Overall outcome	0%	3%	16%	47%	34%	4.1	–
Ability to think in new ways	0%	5%	17%	48%	29%	4.0	3.5
	1: Do not agree	2	3	4	5: Completely agree		
This method is an effective way of learning	0%	5%	14%	29%	52%	4.3	–
To learn by teaching is a teaching method that I will use with my students in school	0%	7%	10%	22%	60%	–	–

The national mean result covers the whole teacher education program, including teaching practice and campus teaching in pedagogy and subject didactics. It is used as a benchmark in the present study. See Chapter 2 for more information.

Table A.3 Development of teaching skills (percentage frequency distribution)

(N = 58)	1: Not satisfied	2	3	4	5: Very satisfied	Mean	National mean
1. Vocational and subject-specific skills	2%	5%	36%	31%	26%	3.8	3.5
2. Collaborative skills	2%	5%	14%	41%	38%	4.1	4.1
3. Peers' ability to give constructive feedback on your work	0%	14%	21%	43%	22%	3.7	3.4

Table A.4 Student motivation (percentage frequency distribution)

(N = 58)	1: Not satisfied	2	3	4	5: Very satisfied	Mean	National mean
Your motivation to do this type of teaching	0%	7%	17%	40%	36%	4.1	3.1* Item: The study program contributes to your study motivation
	1: Do not agree				5: Completely agree		
The teaching is designed to allow us to be active participants	0%	3%	16%	29%	52%	4.3	3.5
My peers make their teaching engaging	0%	9%	10%	43%	38%	4.1	3.2* Item: The faculty staff makes their teaching engaging

Table A.5 Academic learning (percentage frequency distribution)

(N = 58)	1: Not satisfied	2	3	4	5: Very satisfied	Mean	National mean
Subject matter in pedagogy		5%	22%	45%	28%	3.9	3.5 Theoretical subject matter
Ability to reflect and think critically	0%	3%	17%	48%	29%	4.0	3.9

Second case study

Table A.6 Overall learning from peer teaching (percentage frequency distribution)

(N = 92)	1: No benefit at all	2	3	4	5: Very large benefit	Mean std. deviation
"Overall, how much have you learned from peer teaching?"	6	16	44	30	4	3.1 (0.92)

Table A.7 Overall learning by being a peer teacher

(N = 92) percentage frequency distribution	1: No benefit at all				Very large benefit	Mean std. deviation
"How have you experienced the learning outcome of Assignment 1? (peer teaching with written reflection text?)"	2	17	30	38	12	3.4 (0.98)

Table A.8 Student perceptions of peer teacher learning (percentage frequency distribution)

(N = 92): Please respond to the following statements about the role of a peer teacher	1: Strongly disagree	2: Somewhat disagree	3: Neither agree nor disagree	4: Somewhat agree	5: Strongly agree	Mean score (std. deviation)
"I have gained a very significant academic learning outcome from being a peer teacher myself"	10	17	37	27	9	3.1 (1.09)
"I have gained a lot of relevant teaching experience from being a student teacher"	12	26	25	30	7	2.9 (1.15)
"I have been extremely motivated in relation to conducting peer teaching"	19	21	28	25	8	2.8 (1.23)

(Continued)

Table A.8 (Continued)

(N = 92): Please respond to the following statements about the role of a peer teacher	1: Strongly disagree	2: Somewhat disagree	3: Neither agree nor disagree	4: Somewhat agree	5: Strongly agree	Mean score (std. deviation)
"I have had a great deal of performance anxiety related to conducting student-led teaching"	40	19	21	16	4	2.3 (1.26)
"I have found it very enjoyable to choose the types of tasks the students will work with"	5	10	32	44	10	3.4 (0.99)
"I have found it very enjoyable to lead the whole-class discussion with the students"	11	18	49	16	7	2.9 (1.02)
"I have had a great interest in the subject matter I have taught"	10	19	44	22	6	3.0 (1.02)
"I think the cooperation with the other peer teachers has worked very well"	1	3	7	41	48	4.3 (0.8)
"I experience a high degree of accomplishment after conducting peer teaching"	6	11	39	25	20	3.4 (1.01)

Table A.9 Student perceptions of the importance of peer teaching (percentage frequency distribution)

(N = 92)	1: Not important	2:	3:	4:	5: Very important
"How important is it that student teachers do peer teaching in teacher education?"	10	14	34	25	10

Table A.10 Perceived stress by being a peer teacher

"How does it feel to stand in front of your peers as a class compared to standing in front of school students?"	Percentage distribution
Much more stressful to stand in front of peers than in front of students	24
Slightly more stressful to stand in front of peers than in front of students	49
About the same in terms of stress level	23
Slightly less stressful to stand in front of peers than in front of students	2
Much less stressful to stand in front of peers than in front of students	2

Table A.11 Perceived relevance of peer teaching (percentage frequency distribution)

(N = 91) As a student participant, how relevant has the peer teaching been for:	1: Not relevant at all	2	3	4	5: Very relevant	Mean (std. deviation)
your future job as a teacher	4	24	36	25	10	3.1 (1.03)
processing the subject matter or syllabus in your studies	8	23	34	30	6	3.0 (1.03)
the semester paper	7	22	30	26	15	3.2 (1.15)

Table A.12 Perceived outcomes of participating in peer teaching (percentage frequency distribution)

(N = 91) Please respond to the following statements about participating in peer teaching	1: Strongly disagree	2: Somewhat disagree	3: Neither agree nor disagree	4: Somewhat agree	5: Strongly agree	Mean score (std. deviation)
I have experienced being a participant in a professional learning community in the seminar group	2	6	26	45	21	3.8 (0.92)
I have been an engaged participant in these lessons	3	6	30	46	15	3.7 (0.92)

(Continued)

Table A.12 (Continued)

(N = 91) Please respond to the following statements about participating in peer teaching	1: Strongly disagree	2: Somewhat disagree	3: Neither agree nor disagree	4: Somewhat agree	5: Strongly agree	Mean score (std. deviation)
I think the quality of the relationship between the students has been very good		8	23	44	26	3.9 (0.89)
I think there has been a very unfair distribution of workload in the class	17	26	20	29	9	2.9 (1.25)
I think the teaching has addressed central questions related to the teaching profession	3	10	19	50	19	3.7 (0.99)
I think this teaching is better than traditional seminar teaching with a teacher educator	15	21	32	22	10	2.9 (1.20)

Table A.13 Perceived outcomes of observational learning in peer teaching (percentage frequency distribution)

(N = 92) In relation to the learning in the seminar group, how would you assess the learning outcome of the following types of observation	1: No benefit at all	2	3	4	5: Very large benefit	Mean std. deviation
Observing how your fellow students teach	7	26	26	35	7	3.1 (1.07)
Observing the diversity of different pedagogical methods	4	16	27	45	8	3.4 (0.99)
Observing and comparing variations in different teaching qualities	5	15	32	38	10	3.3 (1.03)

Table A.14 Perception of the quality of the class environment (percentage frequency distribution)

(N = 91)	1: Not good at all	2	3	4	5: Very good	Mean (std. deviation)
How would you rate the class environment in your seminar group this semester?	1		5	20	44	30	3.9 (0.91)

Table A.15 Perceived learning outcome of receiving peer feedback (percentage frequency distribution)

(N = 91)	1: No learning outcome	2	3	4	5: Very good learning outcome	Mean (std. deviation)
How have you experienced the learning outcome from receiving feedback from students in peer teaching?	24	29	32	11	4	2.4 (1.10)

Table A.16 Perceived learning outcome of peer teaching split on the four different seminar groups. (Mean score)

Items	Seminar group nr. 1 (N = 24)	Seminar group nr. 2 (N = 25)	Seminar group nr. 3 (N = 25)	Seminar group nr. 4 (N = 17)
"Overall, how much have you learned from peer teaching?"	3.1	3.2	3.2	2.8
"How have you experienced the learning outcome of Assignment 1?" (peer teaching with written reflection text?)	3.3	3.4	3.7	3.1
How would you rate the class environment in your seminar group this semester?	3.7	4.6	4.1	3.2
I think the quality of the relationship between the students has been very good	3.8	4.3	4.0	3.4
I have been an engaged participant in these lessons	3.4	3.8	3.8	3.4
Participation and its relevance for "your future job as a teacher"	3.1	3.3	3.2	2.8
Participation and its relevance for learning about the subject matter (syllabus)	3.0	3.1	3.3	2.4

(Continued)

Table A.16 (Continued)

Items	Seminar group nr. 1 (N = 24)	Seminar group nr. 2 (N = 25)	Seminar group nr. 3 (N = 25)	Seminar group nr. 4 (N = 17)
Participation and its relevance for the semester paper	3.5	3.4	3.2	2.5
I have experienced being a participant in a professional learning community in the seminar group	3.8	4.1	3.7	3.3
How have you experienced the learning outcome from receiving feedback from students in peer teaching?	2.4	2.7	2.6	1.8

References

Ab Murat, N. B. (2018). Learning through teaching and sharing in the jigsaw classroom. *Annals of Dentistry University of Malaya, 15*(2), 71–76.

Allen, D. W., Cooper, J. M., & Poliakoff, L. (1972). *Microteaching.* US Department of Health, Education, and Welfare, Office of Education.

Ames, H., Glenton, C., & Lewin, S. (2019). Purposive sampling in a qualitative evidence synthesis: A worked example from a synthesis on parental perceptions of vaccination communication. *BMC Medical Research Methodology, 19*(1), 1–9.

Argyris, C. (1991). Teaching smart people how to learn. *Harvard Business Review, 69*(3), 99–109.

Argyris, C., & Schon, D. A. (1992). *Theory in practice: Increasing professional effectiveness.* John Wiley & Sons.

Argyris, C., & Schön, D. A. (1997). Organizational learning: A theory of action perspective. *Reis,* (77/78), 345–348.

Arsal, Z. (2015). The effects of microteaching on the critical thinking dispositions of pre-service teachers. *Australian Journal of Teacher Education (Online), 40*(3), 140–153.

Aslan, S. (2015). Is learning by teaching effective in gaining 21st century skills? The views of pre-service science teachers. *Educational Sciences: Theory & Practice, 15*(6), 1441–1457.

Aslan, S. (2017a). The effect of learning by teaching on pre-service science teachers' attitudes towards chemistry. *Journal of Turkish Science Education, 14*(3), 1–15.

Aslan, S. (2017b). Learning by teaching: Can it be utilized to develop inquiry skills? *Journal of Education and Training Studies, 5*(12), 190–198.

Bakır, S. (2014). The effect of microteaching on the teaching skills of pre-service science teachers. *Journal of Baltic Science Education, 13*(6), 789–801.

Baltzersen, R. K. (2010). Radical transparency: Open access as a key concept in wiki pedagogy. *Australasian Journal of Educational Technology, 26*(6), 791–809.

Baltzersen, R. K. (2013a). Expanding the metadiscourse concept in knowledge building. Knowledge Building Summer Institute 2013, Puebla, Mexico.

Baltzersen, R. K. (2013b). The importance of metacommunication in supervision processes in higher education. *International Journal of Higher Education, 2*(2), 128–140. https://doi.org/10.5430/ijhe.v2n2p128

Baltzersen, R. K. (2013c). Metadiscourse in knowledge building: A question about written or verbal metadiscourse. Knowledge Building Summer Institute 2013, Puebla, Mexico.

References

Baltzersen, R. K. (2017). *Collective knowledge advancement as a pedagogical practice in teacher education. An explorative case study of student group work with wiki assignments in the interplay between an offline and a global online setting* [Dissertation, University of Oslo, Faculty of Educational Studies.]. Oslo.

Baltzersen, R. K. (2022). *Cultural-historical perspectives on collective intelligence. Patterns in problem solving and innovation.* Cambridge University Press.

Bargh, J. A., & Schul, Y. (1980). On the cognitive benefits of teaching. *Journal of Educational Psychology, 72*(5), 593.

Baricaua Gutierez, S. (2016). Building a classroom-based professional learning community through lesson study: Insights from elementary school science teachers. *Professional Development in Education, 42*(5), 801–817.

Benware, C. A., & Deci, E. L. (1984). Quality of learning with an active versus passive motivational set. *American Educational Research Journal, 21*(4), 755–765.

Black, P., & Wiliam, D. (1998). Assessment and classroom learning. *Assessment in Education: Principles, Policy & Practice, 5*(1), 7–74. https://doi.org/10.1080/0969595980050102

Bowman-Perrott, L., Davis, H., Vannest, K., Williams, L., Greenwood, C., & Parker, R. (2013). Academic benefits of peer tutoring: A meta-analytic review of single-case research. *School Psychology Review, 42*(1), 39–55.

Bruner, J. (1991). The narrative construction of reality. *Critical Inquiry, 18*(1), 1–21.

Cavanaugh, S. (2022). Microteaching: Theoretical origins and practice. *Educational Practice and Theory, 44*(1), 23–40.

Cazden, C. B. (2001). *Classroom discourse: The language of teaching and learning* (2nd ed.). Heinemann.

CECA (International Committee of Museum Educators) Conference Jerusalem, Israel. https://www.exploratorium.edu/education/ifi/constructivist-learning

Comenius, J. A. (1896). *The Great Didactic of John Amos Comenius* (M. W. Keatinge, Trans.). Adam and Charles Black. https://archive.org/details/greatdidacticofj00come/mode/2up

Crouch, C. H., Watkins, J., Fagen, A. P., & Mazur, E. (2007). Peer instruction: Engaging students one-on-one, all at once. *Research-Based Reform of University Physics, 1*(1), 40–95.

Csikszentmihalyi, M. (1990). *Flow: The psychology of optimal experience.* Harper & Row.

Darling-Hammond, L. (2006). Constructing 21st-century teacher education. *Journal of Teacher Education, 57*(3), 300–314.

Dreyfus, H. L., & Dreyfus, S. E. (2005). Peripheral vision: Expertise in real world contexts. *Organization Studies, 26*(5), 779–792.

Duran, D. (2017). Learning-by-teaching. Evidence and implications as a pedagogical mechanism. *Innovations in Education and Teaching International, 54*(5), 476–484.

Duran, D., & Topping, K. (2017). *Learning by teaching: Evidence-based strategies to enhance learning in the classroom.* Routledge.

Duran Gisbert, D., & Monereo Font, C. (2008). The impact of peer tutoring on the improvement of linguistic competence, self-concept as a writer and pedagogical satisfaction. *School Psychology International, 29*(4), 481–499.

Engeström, Y. (2014). *Learning by expanding: An activity-theoretical approach to developmental research* (2nd ed.). Cambridge University Press.

Ericsson, K. A. (2008). Deliberate practice and acquisition of expert performance: A general overview. *Academic Emergency Medicine, 15*(11), 988–994.

References

Ericsson, K. A., Krampe, R. T., & Tesch-Römer, C. (1993). The role of deliberate practice in the acquisition of expert performance. *Psychological Review, 100*(3), 363.

Evans, D. J., & Cuffe, T. (2009). Near-peer teaching in anatomy: An approach for deeper learning. *Anatomical Sciences Education, 2*(5), 227–233.

Falchikov, N. (2001). *Learning together: Peer tutoring in higher education*. Psychology Press.

Fiorella, L., & Kuhlmann, S. (2020). Creating drawings enhances learning by teaching. *Journal of Educational Psychology, 112*(4), 811.

Fiorella, L., & Mayer, R. E. (2013). The relative benefits of learning by teaching and teaching expectancy. *Contemporary Educational Psychology, 38*(4), 281–288.

Fiorella, L., & Mayer, R. E. (2016). Eight ways to promote generative learning. *Educational Psychology Review, 28*(4), 717–741.

Flavell, J. H. (1979). Metacognition and cognitive monitoring: A new area of cognitive–developmental inquiry. *American Psychologist, 34*(10), 906.

Freire, P. (2005). *Pedagogy of the oppressed*. The Continuum International Publishing Group Inc. https://envs.ucsc.edu/internships/internship-readings/freire-pedagogy-of-the-oppressed.pdf

Gallagher, S. E., & Savage, T. (2020). Challenge-based learning in higher education: An exploratory literature review. *Teaching in Higher Education, 0*, 1–23.

Gazula, S., McKenna, L., Cooper, S., & Paliadelis, P. (2017). A systematic review of reciprocal peer tutoring within tertiary health profession educational programs. *Health Professions Education, 3*(2), 64–78.

Hanke, U. (2012). Learning by teaching. In N. M. Seel (Ed.), *Encyclopedia of the sciences of learning* (pp. 1830–1832). Springer.

Harlen, W., Crick, R. D., Broadfoot, P., Daugherty, R., Gardner, J., James, M., & Stobart, G. (2002). *A systematic review of the impact of summative assessment and tests on students' motivation for learning*. Faculty of Social Sciences Research Reports. EPPI-Centre, University of London.

Hattie, J. (2009). *Visible learning: A synthesis of over 800 meta-analyses relating to achievement*. Routledge.

Hattie, J. (2023, March 26). Education expert John Hattie's new book draws on more than 130,000 studies to find out what helps students learn. *The Conversation*. https://theconversation.com/education-expert-john-hatties-new-book-draws-on-more-than-130-000-studies-to-find-out-what-helps-students-learn-201952

Hein, G. E. (1991, October 15–22). *Constructivist learning theory*. The Museum and the Needs of People.

Henington, C., & Skinner, C. H. (1998). Peer monitoring. In K. Topping & S. Ehly (Eds.), *Peer assisted learning* (pp. 237–253). Routledge.

Henze, R. C. (1992). *Informal teaching and learning: A study of everyday cognition in a Greek community*. Routledge.

Johnson, D. W. (1994). *Cooperative learning in the classroom*. ERIC.

Johnson, D. W., & Johnson, R. T. (2018). Cooperative learning: The foundation for active learning. In S. M. Brito (Ed.), *Active learning—beyond the future*. IntechOpen. https://doi.org/10.5772/intechopen.81086

Kobayashi, K. (2019). Interactivity: A potential determinant of learning by preparing to teach and teaching. *Frontiers in Psychology, 9*, 2755.

Kobayashi, K. (2021a). Effects of collaborative versus individual preparation on learning by teaching. *Instructional Science, 49*(6), 811–829. https://doi.org/10.1007/s11251-021-09561-6

Kobayashi, K. (2021b). Learning by teaching face-to-face: The contributions of preparing-to-teach, initial-explanation, and interaction phases. *European Journal of Psychology of Education.* https://doi.org/10.1007/s10212-021-00547-z

Kokotsaki, D., Menzies, V., & Wiggins, A. (2016). Project-based learning: A review of the literature. *Improving Schools, 19*(3), 267–277.

Kolb, D. A. (2015). *Experiential learning: Experience as the source of learning and development* (2nd ed.). Pearson Education.

Lave, J., & Wenger, E. (1991). *Situated learning: Legitimate peripheral participation.* Cambridge University Press.

Letrud, K., & Hernes, S. (2018). Excavating the origins of the learning pyramid myths. *Cogent Education, 5*(1), 1518638. https://doi.org/10.1080/2331186X.2018.1518638

Leung, K. C. (2015). Preliminary empirical model of crucial determinants of best practice for peer tutoring on academic achievement. *Journal of Educational Psychology, 107*(2), 558.

Leung, K. C. (2019). An updated meta-analysis on the effect of peer tutoring on tutors' achievement. *School Psychology International, 40*(2), 200–214.

Lockspeiser, T. M., O'Sullivan, P., Teherani, A., & Muller, J. (2008). Understanding the experience of being taught by peers: The value of social and cognitive congruence. *Advances in Health Sciences Education, 13*(3), 361–372.

Loda, T., Erschens, R., Loenneker, H., Keifenheim, K. E., Nikendei, C., Junne, F., Zipfel, S., & Herrmann-Werner, A. (2019). Cognitive and social congruence in peer-assisted learning–A scoping review. *PLoS One, 14*(9), e0222224.

Martin, J.-P. (2018). Lernen durch Lehren: Konzeptualisierung als Glücksquelle. In O.-A. Burow & S. Bornemann (Eds.), *Das große Handbuch Unterricht & Erziehung in der Schule* (pp. 345–360). Carl Link Verlag.

Maslow. (1981). *Motivation and personality.* Prabhat Prakashan.

Masters, K. (2013). Edgar Dale's Pyramid of Learning in medical education: A literature review. *Medical Teacher, 35*(11), e1584–e1593.

Mazur, E. (1997). *Peer instruction. A user's manual.* Prentice Hall.

Moust, J., Bouhuijs, P., & Schmidt, H. (2021). *Introduction to problem-based learning: A guide for students.* Routledge.

Moust, J. H., & Schmidt, H. G. (1994). Facilitating small-group learning: A comparison of student and staff tutors' behavior. *Instructional Science, 22*(4), 287–301.

Nottingham, J. (2015). *Challenging learning: Theory, effective practice and lesson ideas to create optimal learning in the classroom.* Routledge.

Palinscar, A. S., & Brown, A. L. (1984). Reciprocal teaching of comprehension-fostering and comprehension-monitoring activities. *Cognition and Instruction, 1*(2), 117–175.

Parker, K. (2023, January 11). John Hattie: Why teaching strategies don't make you an expert teacher. *TES Magazine.* https://www.tes.com/magazine/teaching-learning/general/john-hattie-visible-learning-teaching-strategies-dont-make-you-expert

Patton, M. Q. (2014). *Qualitative research & evaluation methods: Integrating theory and practice.* Sage Publications.

Puchner, L. D. (2003, April 21–25). *Children teaching for learning: What happens when children teach others in the classroom?* Annual Meeting of the American Educational Research Association, Chicago, IL.

Ralph, E. G. (2014). The effectiveness of microteaching: Five years' findings. *International Journal of Humanities Social Sciences and Education, 1*(7), 17–28.

Rees, E. L., Quinn, P. J., Davies, B., & Fotheringham, V. (2016). How does peer teaching compare to faculty teaching? A systematic review and meta-analysis. *Medical Teacher*, *38*(8), 829–837.
Roscoe, R. D. (2014). Self-monitoring and knowledge-building in learning by teaching. *Instructional Science*, *42*(3), 327–351.
Roscoe, R. D., & Chi, M. T. (2008). Tutor learning: The role of explaining and responding to questions. *Instructional Science*, *36*(4), 321–350.
Sander, R., & Bambauer, J. (2012). The secret of my success: How status, eliteness, and school performance shape legal careers. *Journal of Empirical Legal Studies*, *9*(4), 893–930. https://doi.org/10.1111/j.1740-1461.2012.01267.x
Sawyer, R. K. (2006). *Explaining creativity: The science of human innovation*. Oxford University Press.
Sawyer, R. K. (2022). An introduction to the learning sciences. In R. K. Sawyer (Ed.), *The Cambridge handbook of the learning sciences* (3rd ed., pp. 1–24). Cambridge University Press. https://doi.org/10.1017/9781108888295.002
Scardamalia, M., & Bereiter, C. (2006). Knowledge building: Theory, pedagogy, and technology. In R. K. Sawyer (Ed.), *The Cambridge handbook of the learning sciences* (pp. 97–118). Cambridge University Press.
Scardamalia, M., & Bereiter, C. (2021). Knowledge building: Advancing the state of community knowledge. In U. Cress, C. Rosé, A. F. Wise, & J. Oshima (Eds.), *International handbook of computer-supported collaborative learning* (pp. 261–279). Springer International Publishing. https://doi.org/10.1007/978-3-030-65291-3_14
Schön, D. A. (1984). *The reflective practitioner: How professionals think in action* (Vol. 5126). Basic Books.
Schunk, D. H. (1998). Peer modeling. In K. Topping & S. Ehly (Eds.), *Peer-assisted learning* (pp. 185–202). Routledge.
Sen, A. I. (2009). A study on the effectiveness of peer microteaching in a teacher education program. *Egitim ve Bilim*, *34*(151), 165.
Sfard, A. (1998). On two metaphors for learning and the dangers of choosing just one. *Educational Researcher*, *27*(2), 4–13.
Stahl, G. (2006). *Group cognition: Computer support for building collaborative knowledge*. MIT Press.
Stigmar, M. (2016). Peer-to-peer teaching in higher education: A critical literature review. *Mentoring & Tutoring: Partnership in Learning*, *24*(2), 124–136.
Surowiecki, J. (2005). *The wisdom of crowds: Why the many are smarter than the few*. Abacus.
Thomas, J., & Harden, A. (2008). Methods for the thematic synthesis of qualitative research in systematic reviews. *BMC Medical Research Methodology*, *8*, 45–45. https://doi.org/10.1186/1471-2288-8-45
Topping, K. (1996). The effectiveness of peer tutoring in further and higher education: A typology and review of the literature. *Higher Education*, *32*(3), 321–345.
Topping, K. (2005). Trends in peer learning. *Educational Psychology*, *25*(6), 631–645.
Topping, K. (2009). Peer assessment [Article]. *Theory into Practice*, *48*(1), 20–27. https://doi.org/10.1080/00405840802577569
Topping, K., Buchs, C., Duran, D., & Van Keer, H. (2017). *Effective peer learning: From principles to practical implementation*. Routledge.
Topping, K., & Ehly, S. (1998). *Peer-assisted learning*. Routledge.

Tsevreni, I. (2018). The ignorant environmental education teacher: Students get empowered and teach philosophy of nature inspired by ancient Greek philosophy. *Environmental Education Research*, *24*(1), 67–79. https://doi.org/10.1080/13504622.2016.1249457

Velez, J. J., Cano, J., Whittington, M. S., & Wolf, K. J. (2011). Cultivating change through peer teaching. *Journal of Agricultural Education*, *52*(1), 40–49.

Vosniadou, S. (2020). Students' misconceptions and science education. In *Oxford Research Encyclopedia of Education*. Oxford University Press.

Vygotsky, L. S. (1978). *Mind in society: The development of higher psychological processes*. Harvard University Press.

Wenger, E. (1999). *Communities of practice: Learning, meaning, and identity*. Cambridge University Press.

Whitman, N. A., & Fife, J. D. (1988). *Peer teaching: To Teach is To Learn Twice* (ASHE-ERIC Higher Education Reports, Issue. A. f. t. S. o. H. E. Education & E. C. o. Higher.

Yew, E. H. J., & Goh, K. (2016). Problem-based learning: An overview of its process and impact on learning. *Health Professions Education*, *2*(2), 75–79. https://doi.org/https://doi.org/10.1016/j.hpe.2016.01.004

Zuckerman, G. (2021). The role of peers in the mental development of the child. *Journal of Russian & East European Psychology*, *58*(5–6), 318–347.

Index

Note: **Bold** page numbers refer to tables.

assessment, formal 44, 48, 59, 75, 86–87, 91, 100; *see also* exam

collaboration 7, 47, 71; rule-governed **6**, 106
collective intelligence 12, 106–114; as environmental sensing 112; as rotation 93, 95, 102, 106–107
Comenius, John Amos 1–2
communality 19, 27, 37, 96; class atmosphere 19, 37, 38, 63–64, 96
community of learners 37, 50, 95, 107–108; professional learning community 56, 61, 62, 71, 100, 103
competence: innovation 105; social 11; vocational 30, 70; *see also* teaching proficiency
congruence 22–25, 88
constructivism 81
creativity 11
critical thinking 43, 92, 100–101
crowd wisdom 111, 114
deliberative practice 70

democracy: ancient Athens 107; citizen assembly 106; as empowerment 95, 100, 108; participation 95, 106
Dewey, John 81
diversity 29, 37, 50, 106, 111–113; learning-from-diversity 113; learning-in-diversity 111–113; lesson 49–50; lesson content 101, 104; quality of the teaching 104–106; relational 107–108; teaching methods 103; teaching styles 102–103, 107; whole-group 101–105

equality 5, 50–51, 107, 109, 114
exam 21, 36, 44, 48, 52, 53, 59, 86–87, 95–96, 98
expertise, citizen 106

fairness 20, 64, 74, 95, 107
feedback 105, 110; anonymous 100; collective peer 63; peer 3, 9, 17, 31, 37, 52–53, 70, 77, 88, 94, 97, 99–101, 108, 110; teacher 17–18, 31, 37, 55, 63, 77, 97, 99–100, 103, 110; whole-group 99–101
free riders 95
Freire, Paulo 108–109

Hattie, John 3

instructional design (parallel vs. sequentialized) 107, 111–114
IRE-communication 66, 69, 87, 103, 113

jigsaw method 5–**6**

knowledge: background 26, 34, 35, 68, 88, 91, 104, 109–110; building 7, 12, 97–98, 110; development of collective 53, 98, 108; narrative 109; practical 84–86; sharing 2, **6**, 37, 62, 98, 108–109; subject matter 4, 35, 81, 86, 89, 98, 109, 112; telling 22, 99; whole-group 96–99

learning: academic 42–45, 58–59, 60, 76, 81, 83–84; of attitudes 11, 32, 34; cooperative 3, 5–**6**, 93; cycle 30, 94, 110; deep 2, 10–11, 27, 29, 33–34, 43, 46–47, 58, 62,

Index

68–69, 77, 80, 102; of failure 105, 113; iterative 75–81; observational 43, 48–51, 53, 62, 93–94, 102–103, 105, 107, 112–113; practice-based 71; professional (*see* teaching proficiency); situated 11, 108
learning by teaching 3; origins 1–2
learning environment 2, 24, 30, 108
learning pyramid 1
learning strategies 22, 34–35, 47, 65, 69, 87, 92; embodied learning 76; generative learning 65–66; metacognition 3, 18, 68–70, 80, 87; minimum strategies 60, 63, 74, 100; repetition 2, 35, 43, 80; summarizing (summary) 5, 7, 28, 29, 35, 40, 43–44, 47, 53, 65, 67–68, 76–77, 86, 98, 102, 104, 109; surface learning 80
lesson: content 84–86; enactment 11, 66, 69, 76, 79; post-lesson phase 77, 79; preparation 11, 29, 36, 47, 60, 69, 71–72, 74–76, 79, 81–82, 104

Martin, Jean Pol 8, 71
mastery *see* self-confidence
microteaching 9, 35, 70–71, 94, 96, 103, 105
misconceptions 29, 31, 36, 66, 84, 91–92, 97, **116**
motivation 2, 22, 28, 42, 59; flow 73; peer teacher 33, 34, 38, 46, 60, 61, 71–75, 80–82

open publishing 99

peer: assessment 3, **6**–7, 110; co-teaching 3, 17–18, 37, 43, 47–48, 60, 71, 80; explanation **6**–7, 66–67, 85, 87, 97; evaluation 9, 110; instruction 97; learning 12; modeling 94
peer learning, collective 11–12, 19–20, 27–28, 30, 36–37, 49–54, 62–64, 93–114
peer student learning 10, 18–19, 21–24, 25–27, 30–31, 35–36, 41–45, 57–59, 83–92
peer teacher learning 10–11, 18, 27, 29–30, 33, 34–35, 45–49, 59–62, 65–82
peer teaching: cross-level 8, 13, 15, 83, 86; definition 3–4; modern research 2–4; formal in smaller groups within the whole group 5–7; formal of the whole group 8–9; informal in smaller groups within the whole group 7; informal of the whole group 7–8; same-level collective 8, 13, 15; typology 5–10
peer tutoring 3–4, 5–6, 9; definition 3–4; reciprocal 5–**6**
performance anxiety 22, 27, 30, 34, 37, 46, 48, 51–52, 60–61, 71–77, 105
pride *see* self-confidence
problem-solving: human swarm 113–114; problem-based learning 85
proximity 88–92; zone of cognitive 90–91; zone of social 91–92

reflection 9, 50, 62, 69, 70, 105, 111; metadiscourse 98, 110; reflective communication 68, 110, 113; reflective practitioners 105; reflective questions 66, 69; verbal metacommunication 80
relations: group 19, 51, 64, 96, 107–108; learning 51, 70
reputation society 110
responsibility; shared 51, 95, 107; social 27, 32–33, 46, 60, 71–72, 81, 96

Schön, Donald 79, 105
self-confidence 11, 22, 26, 30, 32–34, 46, 72–74, 81, 100–101, 105
skills, teaching (*see* teaching proficiency)

teaching: dialogical (*see also* whole-class discussions); engaging 27, 36, 45, 59, 88, 102; reciprocal **6**; standardization 95; "teaching to the test" 36, 44, 53
teaching proficiency 9, 35, 42, 47–48, 57–58, 70, 80, 94, 103

variation 49–50, 63, 80, 101–102, 105, 111–112
videos, instructional 98–99, 109
Vygotsky, Lev 11, 12, 89; germ cell 117; zone of proximate development (ZPD) 89–90

whole-class discussions 60, 66, 69, 72, 74, 76, 87–88, 103
Wikipedia 109–110

For Product Safety Concerns and Information please contact our EU representative GPSR@taylorandfrancis.com
Taylor & Francis Verlag GmbH, Kaufingerstraße 24, 80331 München, Germany

www.ingramcontent.com/pod-product-compliance
Lightning Source LLC
Chambersburg PA
CBHW051751230426
43670CB00012B/2241